D1561248

Facebook API
Developers Guide

WAYNE GRAHAM

Facebook API Developers Guide

Copyright © 2008 by Wayne Graham

All rights reserved. No part of this work may be reproduced or transmitted in any form or by any means, electronic or mechanical, including photocopying, recording, or by any information storage or retrieval system, without the prior written permission of the copyright owner and the publisher.

ISBN-13: 978-1-4302-0969-0

ISBN-10: 1-4302-0969-0

eISBN-13: 978-1-4302-0970-6

Printed and bound in the United States of America (POD)

Trademarked names may appear in this book. Rather than use a trademark symbol with every occurrence of a trademarked name, we use the names only in an editorial fashion and to the benefit of the trademark owner, with no intention of infringement of the trademark.

Lead Editor: Ben Renow-Clarke

Technical Reviewer: Mark Johnson

Editorial Board: Clay Andres, Steve Anglin, Ewan Buckingham, Tony Campbell, Gary Cornell, Jonathan Gennick, Kevin Goff, Matthew Moodie, Joseph Ottinger, Jeffrey Pepper, Frank Pohlmann, Ben Renow-Clarke, Dominic Shakeshaft, Matt Wade, Tom Welsh

Senior Project Manager: Tracy Brown Collins

Copy Editor: Kim Wimpsett

Compositor: Richard Ables

Cover Designer: Kurt Krames

Manufacturing Director: Tom Debolski

Distributed to the book trade worldwide by Springer-Verlag New York, Inc., 233 Spring Street, 6th Floor, New York, NY 10013. Phone 1-800-SPRINGER, fax 201-348-4505, e-mail orders-ny@springer-sbm.com, or visit http://www.springeronline.com.

For information on translations, please contact Apress directly at 2855 Telegraph Avenue, Suite 600, Berkeley, CA 94705. Phone 510-549-5930, fax 510-549-5939, e-mail info//www.apress.com.

Apress and friends of ED books may be purchased in bulk for academic, corporate, or promotional use. eBook versions and licenses are also available for most titles. For more information, reference our Special Bulk Sales—eBook Licensing web page at http://www.apress.com/info/bulksales.

The information in this book is distributed on an "as is" basis, without warranty. Although every precaution has been taken in the preparation of this work, neither the author(s) nor Apress shall have any liability to any person or entity with respect to any loss or damage caused or alleged to be caused directly or indirectly by the information contained in this work.

The source code for this book is available to readers at http://www.apress.com.

For Anna and Stella.

Contents

v

About the Author

WAYNE GRAHAM is the emerging technology and digital library coordinator at the Earl Gregg Swem Library at the College of William and Mary. He has a bachelor's degree in history from the Virginia Military Institute and a master's degree in history from the College of William and Mary. While a graduate student, he worked with the Colonial Williamsburg Foundation on a project digitizing the foundation's collection of books, manuscripts, and research reports and discovered a love of all things technical. After funding for the project ran out, Wayne took a position at William and Mary where he works to find new ways to integrate new technology into the library and helps scholars from across the country develop online projects for research.

Wayne currently resides in Williamsburg, Virginia, with his wife, Anna; daughter, Stella; and two crazy dogs, Nikki and Jasper. In his "free" time, Wayne enjoys reading, playing almost any video game, and spending quality time with his family. If you're so inclined, you can add Wayne as a friend on Facebook.

About the Technical Reviewer

MARK JOHNSON is a lieutenant in the United States Navy and currently a senior instructor at the U.S. Naval Academy. He has a bachelor's degree from the Naval Academy and a master's degree in computer science from George Washington University.

When not working, Mark enjoys spending time with his wife, Lori, and their friends.

CHAPTER 1

Introducing the Facebook Platform

Facebook (http://www.facebook.com) has grown phenomenally over the past several years from an Ivy League social web application to the second largest social web site on the Internet. The creators of Facebook have done an impressive job focusing their social software on the college demographic. In a natural progression of the social network, Facebook recently extended its network by developing a platform for developers to create new applications to allow Facebook users to interact in new and exciting ways.

What Is Facebook?

In 2007, Facebook launched its own platform for application development. The platform consists of an HTML-based markup language called Facebook Markup Language (FBML), an application programming interface (API) for making representational state transfer (REST) calls to Facebook, a SQL-styled query language for interacting with Facebook called Facebook Query Language (FQL), a scripting language called Facebook JavaScript for enriching the user experience, and a set of client programming libraries. Generically, the tools that make up the Facebook platform are loosely called the Facebook API.

By releasing this platform, Facebook built an apparatus that allows developers to create external applications to empower Facebook users to interact with one another in new and exciting ways—ways that you, as a developer, get to invent. Not only can you develop web applications, but Facebook has also opened up its platform to Internet-connected desktop applications with its Java client library. By opening this platform up to both web-based and desktop applications and offering to general users the same technology that Facebook developers use to build applications, Facebook is positioning itself to be a major player in the future of socio-technical development.

A Brief History of Facebook

In 2003, eUniverse launched a new social portal called MySpace. This web site became wildly popular very quickly, reaching the 20-million-user mark within a year. Just a year earlier, a bright young programmer named Mark Zuckerberg matriculated at Harvard University. The year in which MySpace launched, Zuckerberg and his friend Adam D'Angelo launched a new media player, called Synapse, that featured the Brain feature. Synapse's Brain technology created playlists from your library by picking music that you like more than music than you don't. Although this type of smart playlist generation is common in today's media players, at its launch, it was an innovation. Synapse's launch was met with positive reviews, and several companies showed interest in purchasing the software; however, ultimately no deals were made, and the media player never took off.

Unfortunately (or fortunately, depending on your perspective), one of Zuckerman's next projects created quite a bit more controversy. He created Facemash.com, a variant of the HOTorNOT.com web site for Harvard students. To acquire images for the web site, Zuckerberg harvested images of students from the many residence hall web sites at Harvard. Because Zuckerberg was running a for-profit web site and had not obtained students' permission to use their images, Zuckerberg was brought before the university's administrative board on charges of breaching computer security and violating Internet privacy and intellectual property policies. Zuckerberg took a leave of absence from Harvard after the controversy and then relaunched his site as a social application for Harvard students in 2004. The viral nature of the web site allowed it to grow quickly, and a year later Zuckerberg officially withdrew from Harvard to concentrate his efforts on developing what was first known as thefacebook.com.

Relaunched as Facebook in 2005, the social network quickly expanded to the rest of the Ivy League. Soon after, Facebook expanded dramatically across university and college campuses across the nation. Facebook's focus on the college and university demographic helped catapult it into what any marketing manager will tell you is the most difficult demographic to crack, the 18–24 young adult market.

To keep its growing momentum, Facebook opened its doors to nonacademic users for the first time in 2007. Since this time, Facebook has grown to be the second largest social network with more than 30 million users. And with any growth comes opportunities both for the company and for its users.

The Elements of the Facebook Platform

As stated previously, the Facebook platform consists of five components: a markup language derived from HTML (Facebook Markup Language), a REST API for handling communication between Facebook and your application, a SQL-style language for interacting with Facebook data (Facebook Query Language), a scripting language (Facebook JavaScript), and a set of client libraries for different programming languages. I'll cover these five elements in the following sections.

Facebook Markup Language

If you've ever developed in ColdFusion or JSTL (or other tag-based programming language), you'll find working with the platform's Facebook Markup Language (FBML) very natural. If you're new to tag-based programming, just think of FBML as fancy HTML tags, because each interaction starts and ends with a tag. However, to distinguish between HTML and Facebook commands, you prefix the tags with fb: as you would if you were using multiple DTDs/schemas in XHTML. By using the FBML tag set, Facebook abstracts a lot of complex code and makes many of the routine procedures almost effortless. For example, to add a link to your application's help pages on your dashboard (the navigational tabs that go across the top), you simply need to add the following lines:

```
<fb:dashboard>
    <fb:help href="help.php">Application Help</fb:help>
</fb:dashboard>
```

REST API Calls

Facebook API calls are grouped into eight action categories. These calls are really wrappers for more sophisticated FQL interactions with the Facebook back end but are useful bits of code that speed up the development of your application. These calls include the following:

- facebook.auth provides basic authentication checks for Facebook users.

- facebook.feed provides methods to post to Facebook news feeds.

- facebook.friends provides methods to query Facebook for various checks on a user's friends.

- facebook.notifications provides methods to send messages to users.

- facebook.profile allows you to set FBML in a user's profile.

- facebook.users provides information about your users (such as content from the user's profile and whether they are logged in).

- facebook.events provides ways to access Facebook events.

- facebook.groups provides methods to access information for Facebook groups.

- facebook.photos provides methods to interact with Facebook photos.

Facebook Query Language

The Facebook Query Language (FQL) is a SQL-style language specifically designed to allow developers to interact with Facebook information. Facebook allows you to interact with nine separate "tables" to query information directly. You have access to the following:

- user
- friend
- group
- group_member
- event
- event_member
- photo
- album
- phototag

I'll get into the specifics of the information you have access to in these "tables" later in the book, but suffice to say, Facebook exposes a lot of information to you for your application. And, like most SQL implementations, some additional functions allow you to take a few shortcuts when you request user information:

- now() returns the current time.
- strlen(string) returns the length of the string passed to the function.
- concat(string1, string2,…, stringN) concatenates N strings together.
- substr(string, start, length) returns a substring from a given string.
- strpos(haystack, needle) returns the position of the character needle in the string haystack.
- lower(string) casts the given string to lowercase.
- upper(string) casts the given string to uppercase.

To write FQL, you follow basic SQL syntax. For example, to extract my name and picture from Facebook, you would write a simple query like so:

```
SELECT name, pic
FROM user
WHERE uid = 7608007
```

The previous snippet, when executed by the Facebook platform, will return a structure (in a format that you define in your call) with a URL to the image of the profile image for user 7608007. Calls like these are useful in giving you granular control of the information you get back from the API.

Facebook JavaScript

To minimize the threat of cross-site scripting (XSS) attacks, Facebook implemented its own JavaScript for developers who really want, or need, to use JavaScript in their applications. Facebook *scrubs* (removes) much of the JavaScript you can add to your application, but by using Facebook JavaScript (FBJS) you can still enrich the user's experience. Facebook formally released FBJS 1.0 in September 2007. If you're well versed in JavaScript, you'll pick this up quickly (or perhaps find it maddening). The following is a quick example of how you can provide a modal dialog box to your users:

```
<a href="#" onclick="new Dialog().showMessage('Dialog', 'This is the help message
for this link');return false">Show Dialog Box</a>
```

When processed through the Facebook platform, a user will be shown the modal dialog box represented in Figure 1-1 after clicking the Show Dialog Box hyperlink. Not bad for a single line of code!

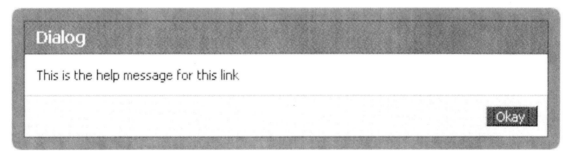

Figure 1-1. Modal dialog box

Client Libraries

The Facebook platform provides many tools to access information, but you are responsible for providing your own business logic through some other language. Facebook facilitates this through "official" client libraries for both PHP and Java that provide convenient methods to access the Facebook application. However, not everyone in the universe uses Java and PHP exclusively. To help the rest of the programmers who want to develop their own Facebook application, client libraries are available for the following languages:

- ActionScript
- ASP.NET
- ASP (VBScript)
- ColdFusion
- C++
- C#
- D
- Emacs Lisp
- Lisp
- Perl
- PHP (4 and 5)
- Python
- Ruby
- VB .NET
- Windows Mobile

This complement of languages should take care of just about most developers today. And although these client libraries are not "officially" supported by Facebook (meaning they won't answer your questions about using them), they are posted by the company with at least some tacit approval of being the "officially unofficial" client libraries. By the way, I'm still waiting for them to include a library for Assembly.

Summary

In this chapter, I briefly went over what the Facebook platform is and outlined some of its technologies and capabilities. I also talked about how Facebook has grown to be the second largest social network on the Web. In the forthcoming chapters, I'll get more into the specifics of what the different parts of the platform do and how these components work together to allow programmers to develop rich applications for Facebook users.

In the next chapter, you'll work on setting up a new application from scratch, including setting up your server. There's not much to set up before you start building your application, but you will need to pay attention to a few things in order to help in your planning and implementation stages.

Graham

CHAPTER 2

Getting Ready for Facebook Application Development

Keeping with its user focus, Facebook makes it easy to both set up and maintain applications. Because your application doesn't live on Facebook's servers, you need to put certain things in place before you start developing. This chapter will cover setting up your environment so you can start coding your application. It will also cover some of the tools that Facebook provides you to help develop and debug your code.

Getting to know a new platform can be daunting, especially one that has so many facets like the Facebook platform. To help you get your feet wet with the different aspects of the platform, Facebook provides you with a couple tools that let you explore the core API functions, test your Facebook Query Language, and see how your Facebook Markup Language will look in the different areas of the Facebook site.

What's Needed

To get up and running with developing an online Facebook application, you need to have three things in place:

- A valid Facebook account

- Access to a web server running a supported middleware language

- The client library for your particular middleware language

If you're working on a desktop application, you still need a Facebook account (for authentication), but you will need only the client library for your language because your interactions with the Facebook servers will be handled by your program and not a web server.

Creating a Facebook Account

Setting up a Facebook account is a simple process. If you don't already have one, don't worry; it's free, and anyone can sign up to use Facebook. Just point your browser to http://www.facebook.com, and click the Sign Up button (see Figure 2-1).

Already a Member? **Login**

Facebook is a **social utility** that **connects you** with the people around you.

Everyone can use Facebook — **Sign Up**

upload photos or **publish notes** · get the **latest news** from your friends · post videos on your profile · tag your friends · use **privacy settings** to control who sees your info · **join a network** to see people who live, study, or work around you

Find your friends ▸

Figure 2-1. The Facebook sign-up screen

The form asks a few simple questions about you and will send you a confirmation e-mail to verify your e-mail address. After you confirm your account, you have the opportunity to join a network. These networks are grouped by academic institutions, locations, and businesses and are at the core of Facebook's social structure's organization. Once you join a network, you are able to access information about the people in that network.

Understanding Facebook Layout and Terms

If you're new to Facebook (or even if you've been using it for a while), it's useful to understand how Facebook names the elements in its layout. Facebook utilizes both two- and three-column layouts for different parts of its site with a header and footer containing global links. Except for the header and footer, users can edit their content layout. This is an important design consideration, because depending on where your content is loaded on a user's page, you need to take into account different widths.

On the far left of all pages, users have access to the different applications they have installed in the navigation bar. By default, only four appear (see Figure 2-2), so, depending on how many applications your user has, your application might not appear in their navigation bar. Obviously, if you're designing an application, you want folks to not only use it but to also have it in a convenient location on their Facebook pages.

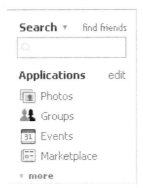

Figure 2-2. The Facebook left navigation box

When users first log in, they are taken to their canvas page. In Facebook-speak, a canvas page is the wide content on the right side of the web page, as shown in Figure 2-3. These pages generally have two- and three-column layouts, with the left application navigation, content in the center pane, and, for three-column layouts, "useful" information on the right such as upcoming birthdays for your friends, invitations to join groups or become friends with individuals, and the ability to update your status (telling your friends what you're doing).

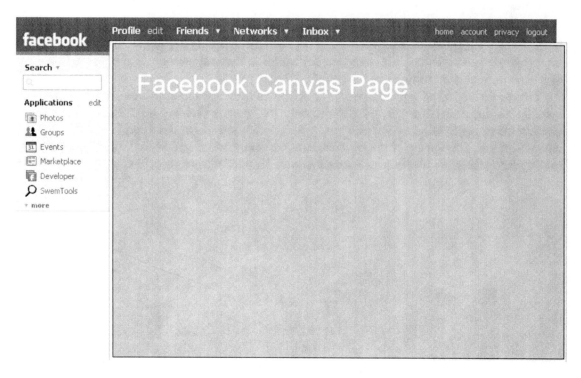

Figure 2-3. The Facebook canvas page

Another important page is the profile page. This is the page you see when you log on to Facebook. The layout on this page is slightly different from the canvas pages. There are still three columns, and the application navigation is still on the left. However, the content column (referred to as *wide*) has shifted to the far right, and it is separated from the application navigation panel by what Facebook calls the *narrow* column. Because users can change the layout of their pages, it's important that you have multiple displays for your application depending on the column in which it's located.

Setting Up Your Server

Since you host your own Facebook application, there is some setup you need to do on your web space. If you don't have a web site (or access to one) that runs PHP, Java, or one of the unsupported languages with a client library, you can use one of the free web hosts available. You will need a middleware application server to handle the business logic for your application because Facebook provides methods only for retrieving data and displaying certain information. I'll be using PHP for the examples in this book, but they should be relatively straightforward to translate into other languages.

Graham

You can download the client libraries for all languages from `http://developer.facebook.com/resources.php`. If you're using a *nix system (including OS X), you can simply do the following:

```
wget http://developers.facebook.com/clientlibs/facebook-platform.tar.gz
tar zxvf facebook-platform.tar.gz
mv facebook-platform <path_to_web_location>
```

The previous snippet moves both the PHP 4 and PHP 5 libraries (along with the Footprints sample application). The PHP 4 library is in the folder php4client, and the PHP 5 library is in the client folder. Most likely you will be working with one library or the other, so you really need to move only one of the folders to your server to work on your application.

Note ➡ Need some hosting? Joyent (`http://www.joyent.com`) recently partnered with Facebook to provide a free year of hosting for Facebook applications (`http://joyent.com/developers/facebook`). There is a waiting list, but it is a pretty good deal for a really good host. Other hosts that have a proven track record with Facebook apps include MediaTemple (`http://www.mediatemple.net`) and Dreamhost (`http://www.dreamhost.com/`). If you're thinking smaller, you might want to try RunHosting (`http://facebook.runhosting.com`) or 110MB (`http://www.110mb.com`). It's good to look at a few and see which one offers the best fit for what you want to do. Many of these web sites also have free database hosting (usually MySQL), which is a great way to get up and running with Facebook application development.

Adding the Developer Application

Once you have an account and have set up a server environment, the next step is to add Facebook's Developer application. Go to `http://www.facebook.com/developers`, and install the application.

Figure 2-4 shows the screen that users are presented with when installing a new application. The check boxes allow certain functionality to be performed by the application, and they give users the ability to turn certain aspects of the application on and off. Once you have read the platform application's terms of use, just click the Add Developer button to install the Developer application.

Graham

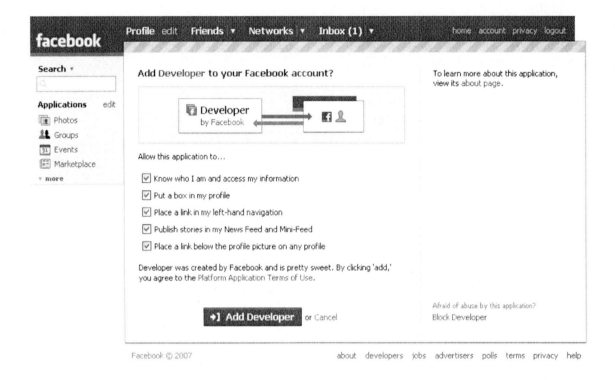

Figure 2-4. Facebook's Developer application installation screen

Once you've installed Developer, you are directed to a Facebook application that helps you manage the applications you are developing, including the most recent entries on the discussion board, news about the Facebook platform, links to your application management interface, and information on the status of the platform (see Figure 2-5).

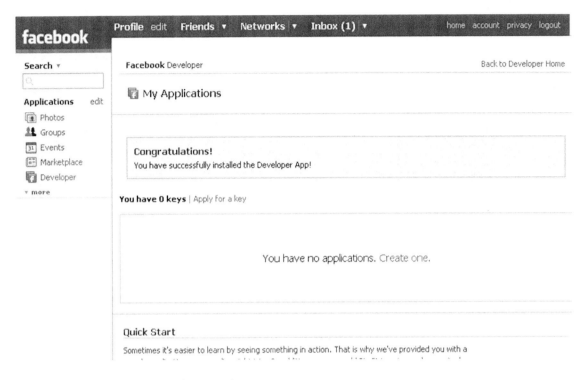

Figure 2-5. Facebook's Developer welcome screen

It's important to keep up-to-date with the platform status because Facebook is adding information about new tags, changes to the terms of service (typically clarifying hazy areas), systemwide outages, and, perhaps most important, platform changes that have the potential to break your application. Like with most things in Facebook, you can subscribe to an RSS feed to help you keep up-to-date with these changes (http://www.facebook.com/feeds/api_messages.php).

Understanding How Facebook Applications Work

Because you host your own application, it's a good idea to go over how Facebook applications actually work. Essentially, Facebook provides your application to users when it is requested through Facebook.

As you can see in Figure 2-6, each time a Facebook user interacts with your application, you set off a series of server interactions with the Facebook server farm and your server. Each time a user requests something from your application through Facebook, that request is passed to your server to create the initial REST call to the Facebook API. Once your server has received the response (in the format you have requested), you server then parses the response to construct a display call (in FBML) and passes that back to the Facebook server. Facebook processes this information and creates an HTML response to the user. Because of the constant passing of information between servers, there is an additional level of complexity that can complicate tracking down bugs. You also need to consider this constant interaction when developing your application because you don't want to make unnecessary API calls that will slow down your application.

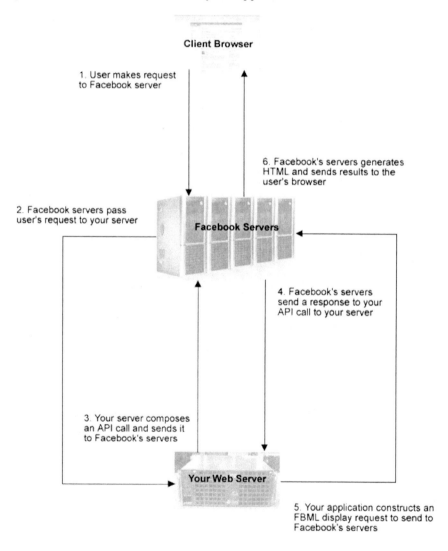

Figure 2-6. Basic Facebook architecture

Graham

Creating a New Application

Now, with all that out of the way, let's set up an application. At this point, you need to tell Facebook about your application. In the Facebook Developer application (http://www.facebook.com/developers), click the Set Up New Application button, as shown in Figure 2-7.

Figure 2-7. Setting up a new application

The only required fields are the application name and the one confirming you have read the terms of service. However, to really do anything with an application, you will need to fill out the optional fields. Don't worry—if you already set up an application and didn't fill out these fields, you can change them by clicking the My Apps link in the Developer application.

Note ➡ You need to remember that you can't use the word *face* anywhere in your application name. Because of this prohibition, you are precluded from using words such as *surface* and *faceted* as part of your application name. A good thesaurus can help you get a bit more creative with your application names.

In the optional fields, you can fill out more information about how your application works (see Figure 2-8). Perhaps the most perplexing field here is the Callback URL field. This is the field that handles your actual application and lives in the server environment you've set up. For example, if you have a web site for your application at http://fake.domain.com/facebookApp, this would be your callback URL.

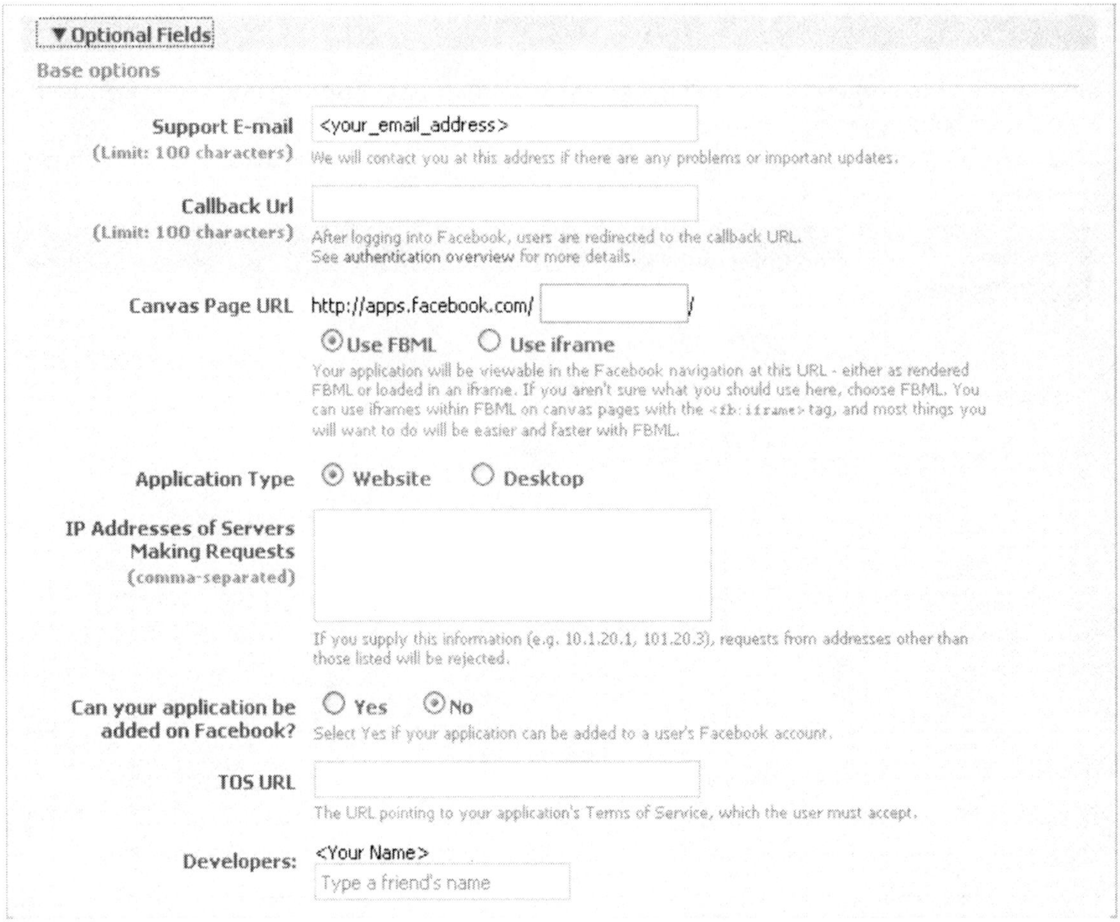

Figure 2-8. Optional fields for Facebook application registration

The following are the optional fields:

Support E-mail: This is the e-mail contact for support questions for your application.

Callback URL: This is the URL of your actual application on your server. If you've set up an application on your server at http://fake.domain.com/facebook_app, that is your callback URL (you'll sometimes see this referred to as the *callback metaphor*).

Canvas Page URL: This is the Facebook URL to your application.

Application Type: Most likely this will be Website, but if you're developing an application in Java (using the official client library) or one of the unofficial libraries that won't be accessed primarily on the Web, select Desktop.

IP Addresses of Servers Making Requests: This is a comma-separated list of servers able to make requests. If you need to lock down your application to a list of servers, this is where you add that information. Requests from other servers are then rejected. If you use this with an online application, the users will be presented with a fatal error in the response stating that an "Unauthorized source IP address" was used to access the application.

Can your application be added on Facebook?: An answer of Yes to this question will allow people to add the application to their account. If you select No, users will be able to use the application but won't be able to add it to their accounts.

TOS URL: This is the URL to the terms of service for your application. If you use this, users must accept the terms of service before they can use your application.

Developers: Your name should appear in this field by default. If you're working with others to develop your application, put their names there too.

Facebook Terms of Service Highlights

Terms of service are something a lot of folks skip over…which they shouldn't. If you're one of these people, please take some time to go over these documents because they're there to save you some headaches in the long run. As with any terms of service agreement, there are certain prohibitions that you should be aware of in terms of what is, and is not, permissible. There have been some recent changes to the Facebook terms of service that are designed to clarify some of the gray areas in the guidelines, and these will most likely continue to change as unscrupulous people look for loopholes.

In an overly simplified version of the terms of service and guidelines, your application shouldn't do anything illegal or encourage anything illegal. You should also not store any more information than you need from your users to make your application function. Almost all the information you need will be available to you with just your user's identification number (UID). And, in case you missed it in the Facebook guidelines and terms of service, you are not permitted to sell your users' information!

Graham

Using Facebook Tools

Facebook provides three important tools for learning and debugging Facebook applications in the Tools section of its Developers web site (`http://developer.facebook.com/tools.php`): the API Test Console, the FBML Test Console, and the Feed Preview Console. Because it's good to have immediate feedback with your code and because it's sometimes difficult to debug coding issues and determine whether the problem exists on your end (of course you would never code a bug!), we'll start our adventure by looking at the test console for both the API calls and FBML.

API Tab

When you first arrive at the Tools page, you are presented with two tabs. The API tab has many of the API calls available to you so you can see what kind of data is being returned. I find it useful in my day-to-day programming to be able to see the data I expect to have returned in order to speed development.

For starters, let's take a look at a simple call to return a list of your friends. Simply select the friends.get option for the Method field. This will return an XML structure with a root element of `<friends_get_response>`. You'll also notice a couple of XML namespaces and a location for the schema. If you run into issues with the responses, remember how you're getting them. If it's XML, you might need to deal with the root XML attributes.

The Facebook API Test Console (Figure 2-9) is a great place to click around and see what different calls will return. Not only can you switch between the different API calls, but you can also change response formats to see what you will get when you change the Response Format field. As you experiment with the different calls, you'll notice that some requests require additional fields. And, if you don't fill out the required fields, Facebook will return error codes in the different response formats. I've listed these in the following sections for your reference.

Figure 2-9. Facebook API Test Console

XML

Here's what the XML result looks like:

```
<?xml version="1.0" encoding="UTF-8"?>
<error_response xmlns="http://api.facebook.com/1.0/"
    xmlns:xsi="http://www.w3.org/2001/XMLSchema-instance"
    xsi:schemaLocation="http://api.facebook.com/1.0/
    http://api.facebook.com/1.0/facebook.xsd">
  <error_code>100</error_code>
  <error_msg>Invalid parameter</error_msg>
  <request_args list="true">
    <arg>
      <key>uids</key>
      <value/>
    </arg>
    <arg>
      <key>fields</key>
      <value/>
    </arg>
    <arg>
      <key>callback</key>
```

```
      <value/>
    </arg>
    <arg>
      <key>app_id</key>
      <value>2227470867</value>
    </arg>
    <arg>
      <key>session_key</key>
      <value>c50b22639edc8d2d0dd29357-7608007</value>
    </arg>
    <arg>
      <key>v</key>
      <value>1.0</value>
    </arg>
    <arg>
      <key>method</key>
      <value>facebook.users.getInfo</value>
    </arg>
    <arg>
      <key>api_key</key>
      <value>0289b21f46b2ee642d5c42145df5489f</value>
    </arg>
    <arg>
      <key>call_id</key>
      <value>1186452883.4263</value>
    </arg>
    <arg>
      <key>sig</key>
      <value>28186e1be6ee4015119a992b638b694a</value>
    </arg>
  </request_args>
</error_response>
```

JSON

JSON uses a slightly different syntax to express the same information:

```
{"error_code":100,
    "error_msg":"Invalid parameter",
    "request_args":[
        {"key":"uids","value":""},
        {"key":"fields","value":""},
        {"key":"callback","value":""},
```

Graham

```
    {"key":"app_id","value":"2227470867"},
    {"key":"session_key","value":"c50b22639edc8d2d0dd29357- 7608007"},
    {"key":"v","value":"1.0"},
    {"key":"format","value":"json"},
    {"key":"method","value":"facebook.users.getInfo"},
    {"key":"api_key","value":"0289b21f46b2ee642d5c42145df5489f"},
    {"key":"call_id","value":"1186452905.8595"},
    {"key":"sig","value":"b7e26b1f71aeffb448d26cdf89f32f6e"}
  ]
}
```

PHP

Here's the PHP:

```
Exception Thrown: FacebookRestClientException
  Code: 100, Message: Invalid parameter
```

You can also try FQL in this box. This is a nice place to start inserting different FQL queries to see what is getting returned in different formats.

Here is a quick sample of FQL that queries Facebook for a link to my profile picture:

```
SELECT pic
FROM user
WHERE uid = 7608007
```

You'll notice the response format returns a single field in the <fql_query_response> element:

```
<?xml version="1.0" encoding="UTF-8"?>
<fql_query_response xmlns="http://api.facebook.com/1.0/"
      xmlns:xsi="http://www.w3.org/2001/XMLSchema-instance"
      list="true">
  <user>
    <pic>http://profile.ak.facebook.com/profile5/1622/61/s7608007_3215.jpg</pic>
  </user>
</fql_query_response>
```

Or, if you prefer to get your responses in JSON, here's the code:

```
[{"pic":"http:\/\/profile.ak.facebook.com\/profile5\/1622\/61\/s7608007_3215.jpg"}]
```

For PHP, here's the code:

```
Array
(
```

Graham

```
[0] => Array
    (
        [pic] =>
         http://profile.ak.facebook.com/profile5/1622/61/s7608007_3215.jpg
    )

)
```

These are all the responses from the same query, just in different response formats. What you'll notice is that each of the formats returns the information in slightly different ways. The XML format is by far the most verbose and, depending on your environment, is something you might want to take into consideration as your calls to the Facebook platform become more complex. Let's look at another FQL query:

```
SELECT first_name, last_name, hometown_location.state, status
FROM user
WHERE uid = 7608007
```

This query will return to you my first and last name, my hometown state, and the status message I set on my home page. This is a basic query that returns a rather straightforward structure. I'll get into some more advanced queries later where you can combine fields and use aggregate functions in FQL to decrease the amount of bandwidth you need to run your applications.

FBML Tab

The Facebook Markup Language is a powerful set of tags that abstracts some rather complex code. Although Facebook will *scrub* (that is, remove) JavaScript you put into your code, it does allow you, through FBML markup, to use certain types of JavaScript code. There are two ways to do this. You can use the MockAjax framework, which you'll find does much of the JavaScripting you need to do, or you can use Facebook JavaScript (FBJS) to let you do more advanced scripting.

Note ➡ In 2005, a "clever" MySpace user figured out how to force people to become his friend by exploiting a hole in their code. Leveraging this vulnerability, the user launched a cross-site scripting (XSS) attack where he was able to add more than 1 million people as friends in the course of a 24-hour period. Because of this type of attack, Facebook restricts the JavaScript available to application developers.

FBML is a superset of HTML, utilizing many of the HTML tags but also adding its own special sauce to allow you to do some rather fun things. To test some of the features you might be considering before you deploy, it's a good idea to see how your code renders when pushed through the Facebook platform.

Again, you can access this tool at `http://developer.facebook.com/tools.php` and click FBML Test Console. Once there, you'll notice a slightly busier interface than the API Test Console (see Figure 2-10).

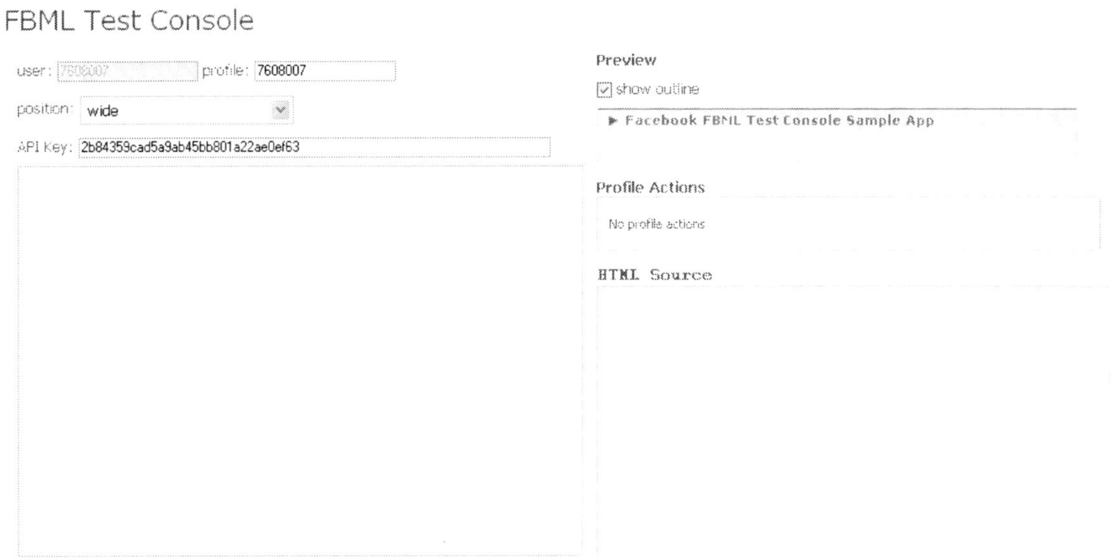

FBML Test Console

user: 7608007 profile: 7608007	Preview
position: wide	☑ show outline
API Key: 2b84359cad5a9ab45bb801a22ae0ef63	▶ Facebook FBML Test Console Sample App
	Profile Actions
	No profile actions
	HTML Source

Figure 2-10. The FBML Test Console

The large panel on the left is where you can type (or paste) your HTML and FBML code and look at the differences in the output (displayed on the right side) for the different positions that you can place your display (narrow, wide, canvas, e-mail, notification, feed title, and feed body). Let's take a look at a couple of simple examples.

First, making the dashboard navigation bar for the top of your application with a set of buttons is a simple task in FBML, as shown by this example from Facebook:

```
<fb:dashboard>

<fb:action href="http://apps.facebook.com/<your_facebook_app>/?id=1234567">
     My Book Reviews
</fb:action>

<fb:action href="http://apps.facebook.com/<your_facebook_app>/new.php">
```

```
      Write a New Review
</fb:action>

<fb:help
    href="http://apps.facebook.com/<your_facebook_app>/help.php"
    title="Need help">
    Help
</fb:help>

<fb:create-button href="http://apps.facebook.com/<your_facebook_app>/new.php">
    Write a New Review
</fb:create-button>

</fb:dashboard>
```

With these few lines of code, you have successfully accomplished the output shown in Figure 2-11.

Figure 2-11. FBML output example

Although we'll get a bit deeper into what's going on here a bit later in the book, I'll discuss a few tags briefly here. The `<fb:dashboard>` tag tells the Facebook platform to consider this a dashboard for the wide panel since this is the default for testing. The `<fb:action>` tags create the two pipe-delimited anchors for "My Book Reviews" and "Write a New Review." The `<fb:help>` tag creates the reference to the help documentation, and the `<fb:create-button>` tag creates the Write a New Review button. You will notice there's some more text here ("Facebook FBML Test Console Sample App"), which Facebook places to help you see what else would be in the "real" application.

You'll also notice that there is some verbose output in the HTML output box. This box illustrates what Facebook translates your FBML input to be for browsers:

```
<div class="dashboard_header">
    <div class="dh_links clearfix">
        <div class="dh_actions">
            <a href="http://apps.facebook.com/<your_facebook_app>/?id=1234567">
                My Book Reviews
            </a>
            <span class="pipe">|</span>
            <a href=" http://apps.facebook.com/<your_facebook_app>/?new.php">
                Write a New Review
            </a>
        </div>
        <div class="dh_help">
            <a href=" http://apps.facebook.com/<your_facebook_app>/?help.php">
                Help
            </a>
        </div>
    </div>
    <div class="dh_titlebar clearfix">
        <h2 style="background-image:

url('http://static.ak.facebook.com/images/icons/hidden.gif?12:27651')">
                Facebook FBML Test Console Sample App
        </h2>
        <div class="dh_new_media_shell">
            <a href=" http://apps.facebook.com/<your_facebook_app>/?new.php"
                class="dh_new_media">
                <div class="tr">
                    <div class="bl">
                        <div class="br">
                            <span>Write a New Review</span>
                        </div>
                    </div>
                </div>
            </a>
        </div>
    </div>
</div>
```

Facebook does a lot behind the scenes to process your application, and it's a good idea to get acquainted with these tools to see what will work (and what won't) before you deploy your application.

Graham

Feed Preview Console Tab

The Feed Preview Console is useful when testing how the information pushed from your application will look when it shows up in the user's feed.

As you can see in Figure 2-12, this console consists of a bunch of text boxes to fill in different parts of the elements for the feed.publishTemplatizedAction API call. This comes in handy when testing the display of the news feeds elements of your code without spamming all your users.

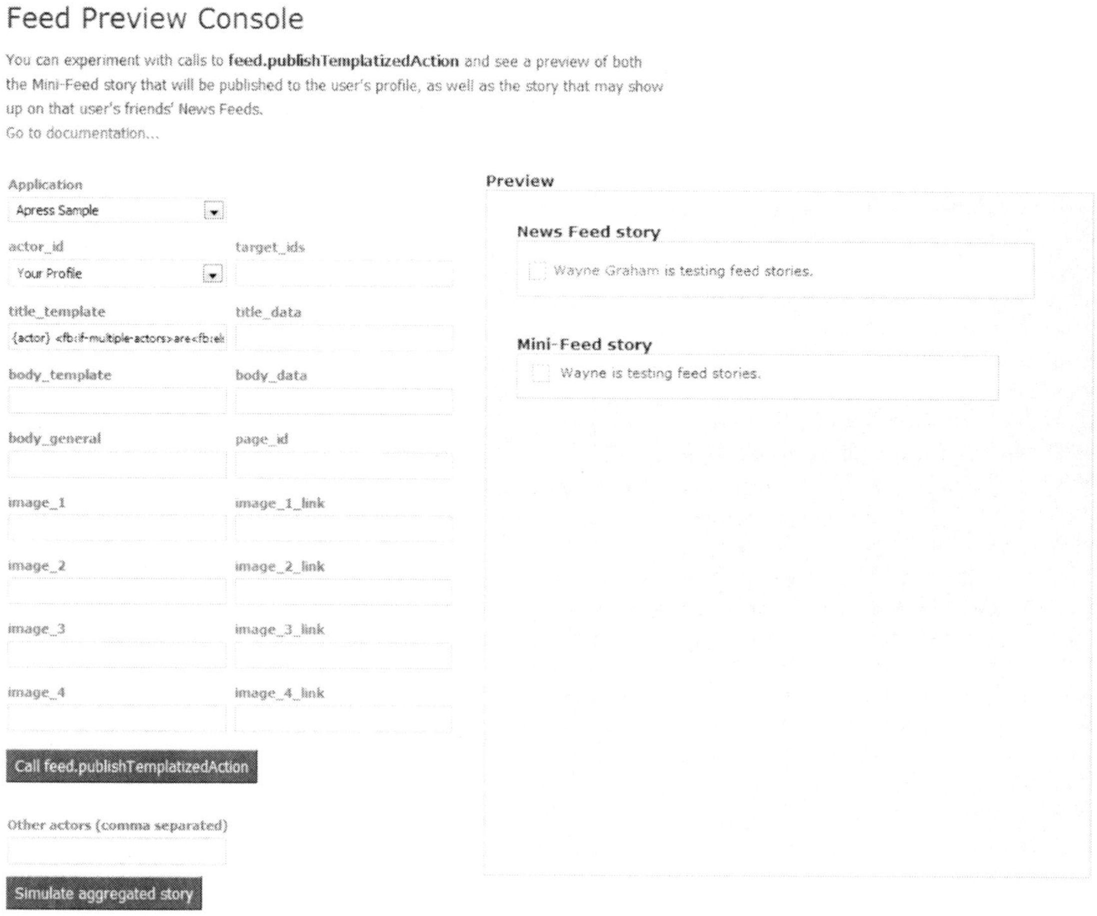

Figure 2-12. The Feed Preview Console

Using Programming Tools

If you don't already have a favorite code editor, finding one can be challenging. Most likely you'll start coding with something as simple as a text editor, but you'll quickly find this to be a pain. Here are some editors that you might want to try to help you with developing your Facebook application:

- Crimson (http://www.crimsoneditor.com/) [Windows]

- ConTEXT (http://www.context.cx/) [Windows]

- Dreamweaver (http://www.adobe.com/products/dreamweaver/) [Windows, OS X]

- Eclipse PDT (http://www.eclipse.org/pdt/) [Windows, OS X, *nix]

- EditPad Lite (http://www.editpadpro.com/editpadlite.html) [Windows]

- Notepad++ (http://notepad-plus.sourceforge.net/uk/site.htm) [Windows]

- phpDesigner (http://www.mpsoftware.dk/) [Windows]

- PhpEd (http://www.nusphere.com/products/phped.htm) [Windows]

- PhpEdit (http://www.waterproof.fr/) [Windows]

- PHP Expert Editor (http://www.ankord.com/phpxedit.html) [Windows]

- Quanta Plus (http://quanta.kdewebdev.org/) [*nix]

- TextMate (http://macromates.com/) [OS X]

One of the nice features of the majority of these editors is that you have the ability to add your own language references. Although there aren't any FBML plug-ins yet for these editors (or at least any that I'm aware of), they could be built very easily.

Summary

This chapter introduced the necessary steps to create a user account on Facebook, to set up your server environment, and to register your yet-to-be developed application with Facebook. It also examined some of the concepts used by Facebook in how it names the different parts of its site and some of the tools that Facebook provides to help you try different parts of the platform (the API Test Console and FBML Test Console). You also briefly looked at how the Facebook platform interprets your code to represent your program to generate HTML for your end users (the Feed Preview Console). It's important to remember that your application is being parsed on at least two servers, the web server your application is hosted on and one of Facebook's servers, before the information gets to your users. You can control only one of those parsers, so code efficiently!

Although you technically could create a Facebook application at this point, it was worth taking a step back and looking at the terminology that the Facebook platform uses for naming elements of pages and some of the tools it provides to help you not only learn about the platform itself but also to help you debug your code!

In the next chapter, you'll take a closer look at the different parts of the Facebook platform and start getting familiar with the syntax Facebook uses. You'll also look at some of the tools Facebook provides to help you get comfortable with the platform as well as try different parts of the platform.

CHAPTER 3

Learning Facebook Platform Fundamentals

As mentioned in Chapter 1, there are five main components of the Facebook platform: API calls, Facebook Markup Language (FBML), Facebook Query Language (FQL), Facebook JavaScript (FBJS), and the client libraries. I consider the client libraries for the various languages to be part of the platform because they are useful abstractions for the specific language in which you are implementing your code. The examples in this chapter will utilize the PHP client library from Facebook, so if you're using a different client library, your syntax will be slightly different. It's important to remember that this chapter is not meant to be an exhaustive reference for the platform (Facebook has a wiki for that at `http://wiki.developers.facebook.com`), but it will cover the major elements you will likely encounter when developing applications.

Client Library Primer

The official client libraries written by Facebook are of the PHP and Java variety. Other language libraries are listed on the Facebook developers web site, but in the interest of simplicity, I'll cover only the PHP library (specifically the PHP 5 library). If you're working with other languages, most of the concepts should be the same, but depending on how the developer who wrote the library chose to implement certain elements (and the characteristics of the language the libraries are being implemented in), the way methods are called and named might be slightly different. As a word of warning, some libraries are better documented than others; some have web sites replete with example code, and others have just a link for a download. If you run into a problem and you can't get help with your language-specific version, take a look at the documentation for the "official" client libraries for PHP or Java.

Facebook's PHP client library consists of two main object classes, Facebook (in `facebook.php`) and FacebookRestClient (in `facebookapi_php5_restlib.php`). As you might expect, the FacebookRestClient class abstracts interactions with Facebook's API. The Facebook class utilizes the FacebookRestClient class's methods to further abstract common interactions with the Facebook platform. For instance, instead of writing a procedure to require a user to have a session key to work with your application, the Facebook object has a method named require_login() that checks for the session key and, if it doesn't find one, redirects the user to Facebook to perform the authentication and then returns the user to your application.

You use the classes just like any other PHP class with require_once (or your other favorite way to create objects):

```php
<?php
/**
 * Include the Facebook PHP client library
 */
    require_once('<path_to_client_library>/facebook.php');

/**
 * Set your API and secret keys
 */
    $api_key    = '<your_api_key>';
    $secret_key = '<your_secret_key>';

/**
 * Initialize a new instance of the Facebook client object
 */
    $facebook = new Facebook($api_key, $secret_key);
?>
```

Your API and secret keys are assigned to you in your My Applications portion of Facebook's Developer application (http://www.facebook.com/developers/apps.php). Once instantiated, the Facebook client libraries make it easy to interact with the Facebook platform.

If you actually look at the code in the library, you'll notice that it contains a few different classes. For instance, when you create a Facebook object, that class is including a library to make the REST calls (facebookapi_php5_restlib.php). If you are using PHP to write a desktop application, the main change is that you would use the facebook_desktop.php file, which extends the Facebook object but is better suited to desktop applications. The facebookapi_php5_restlib.php file is the real workhorse for your application and is where you will find most of the functions you will use in your application.

One nice aspect is that the developers of the Facebook platform used phpDoc conventions, so generating complete documentation for the platform is relatively simple. If you don't have a version of PhpDocumentor, you can download it from SourceForge at http://sourceforge.net/projects/phpdocu/ or use PEAR to install it:

```
pear install PhpDocumentor
```

PEAR should install a new script that you can call from the command-line script, which you then can call to create the documentation:

```
phpdoc -t /path/to/output -d /path/to/facebook_client_library -pp on -ti Facebook
 Client Documentation
```

This line will set the output directory (-t), take a look at the client library path (-d), parse private functions within the code (-pp), set an HTML title of "Facebook Client Documentation" (-ti), and then output the results in HTML using frames. There are many more options for producing documentation, but these options will produce very useful documentation while you develop your Facebook application. For more information about using this tool, check out the phpDocumentor web site at http://www.phpdoc.org/.

API Primer

Facebook has some rather convenient out-of-the box tools for interacting with its back end. At the core of the platform is a set of API calls that wrap more complex code into a single call. In fact, most of the API calls are simply wrappers for complex FQL calls. So, without further adieu, let's take a look at what you have available to you through the API calls.

Facebook's API methods are broken into logical groups of calls. These API calls are also where your first interaction with the platform comes into play. You don't need to use the client library—it just makes things faster since you would need to write these in your language in order to interact with the platform.

To set up the client library for PHP, you simply include the client library in your code. For example, the following snippet makes sure users are logged on to Facebook before displaying a list of the user's friends. Figure 3-1 shows the results.

```php
<?php
/**
 * Set the configuration settings for Facebook
 */
    $facebook_config['debug']      = false;
    $facebook_config['api_key']    = '<your_api_key>';
    $facebook_config['secret_key'] = '<your_secret_key>';
/**
 * include the Facebook client library
 */
    require_once('<path_to_client_library>/facebook.php');

/**
```

```
 * Set up the facebook object
 */
    $facebook = new Facebook($facebook_config['api_key'],
        $facebook_config['secret']);

/**
 * Ensure the user has logged on to Facebook
 */
    $user = $facebook->require_login();

/**
 * Make an API call to call get a user's friends using the PHP library's
 * library
 */

    $friends = $facebook->api_client->friends_get();

    echo "<pre>Friends:" . print_r($friends, true). "</pre>";
?>
```

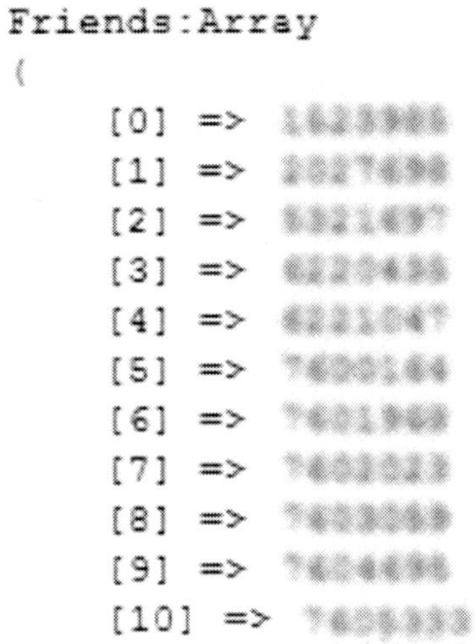

```
Friends:Array
    (
            [0] => 1623986
            [1] => 2027496
            [2] => 5321697
            [3] => 6220436
            [4] => 6221647
            [5] => 7600164
            [6] => 7601969
            [7] => 7603023
            [8] => 7603069
            [9] => 7604496
            [10] => 7605993
```

Figure 3-1. Results of friends_get *API call*

You'll notice a few things in this example. First, you're just throwing the results from the friends object on the screen. I'll cover interacting with the resulting code with FBML a bit later. Second, the syntax for interacting with the API is abstracted into methods in the

Graham

Facebook object. You first set up the Facebook object with the API and secret keys that Facebook assigns to you when you set up your application.

You'll also notice that you require the user to be logged on to Facebook in order to execute the code. This example uses the require_login() method and stores the user's identification number (UID) in the variable user. The next call actually queries the Facebook API method friends.get by wrapping it in the PHP method friends_get. Since the facebook object holds the user's identification number (their primary key or UID), there's no need to pass the UID to the API request. From this short sample code, you can see that the PHP code is actually setting up a REST client to call the facebook.friends.get API method and returns an array of user identifiers:

```
/**
 * Returns the friends of the current session user.
 * @return array of friends
 */
public function friends_get() {
  if (isset($this->friends_list)) {
    return $this->friends_list;
  }
  return $this->call_method('facebook.friends.get', array());
}
```

The client libraries allow you to concentrate on developing your application rather than recoding your interactions with the platform. Since you need to know what you can do with the API, let's take a slightly closer look at the rest of the calls and what they do.

Authentication

The REST API has two methods for dealing with authenticating your users. The method facebook.auth.createToken creates an authentication token (auth_token) that is then passed to the Facebook authentication mechanism. After the user is logged in, the second REST method, facebook.auth.getSession, will contain this token in the response, but only if you specifically request the auth_token in the response.

Authentication is usually (at least when it's done well) a big headache for developing online applications. Because Facebook takes responsibility for these actions, you don't have to purchase SSL certifications, implement your own encryption schema for passwords, or even worry about sessions. In the case of the PHP client library, you start the authentication procedure by calling the Facebook object's require_login method. By calling this method, your users are redirected to Facebook's login pages (https://login.facebook.com/login.php), which are passed your API key, and the user is given a session key and redirected to your callback page. The only difference is that when the user enters the application for the first time, they are asked to accept the terms of service for the application.

Now, you might find yourself in need of performing some task (such as updating FBML), but instead of logging into Facebook every time, you want to update the data to use some sort of scheduled task. You are able to do this with an *infinite* session key.

The process to get your infinite key is a bit convoluted (but, hey, you have to do it only once for each application). After creating your application, create a new page (infinite_key.php) in your callback domain that creates a new Facebook object and echoes your session_key:

```php
<?php

/**
 * @title infinite_key.php
 */

$facebook_config['debug']      = false;
$facebook_config['api_key']    = '<your_api_key>';
$facebook_config['secret_key'] = '<your_secret_key>';

require_once('<path_to_api>/facebook.php');

$facebook = new Facebook($facebook_config['api_key'],
    $facebook_config['secret']);

// force a login page
$user = $facebook->require_login();

$infinate_key = $facebook->api_client->session_key;

echo($infinate_key);

?>
```

Once you have this code on your server, log out of Facebook, clear your Facebook cookies and browser cache (just to make sure nothing funky is going on), and then go to the page you just created on your server (that is, not the application URL, but the actual URL). You will be asked to log on again, so do so, but make sure you check the No Longer Have to Log In to Facebook box. After you've logged on, you should see the infinite key that you can then use in your code.

You can now use your own UID and key in other code to perform anything that needs to happen on a regular basis with the set_user function in the facebook object:

Graham

```
<?php
    ...
    $uid = '<your_uid>';
    $key = '<your infinite key>';

    $facebook->set_user($uid, $key);

    // code that needs to be executed
?>
```

The infinite key is a powerful construct for your Facebook application that you might find you need to implement. Most of the folks who have needed this are updating FBML for features such as mini-feeds or pushing content to their user's profile page.

Events

Event calls have two main wrappers to retrieve information on events. The first, facebook.events.get, returns a response based on the filters passed to it. The second, facebook.events.getMembers, returns the RSVP status for Facebook members for a given event.

FBML

To deal with some of the more advanced features of FBML, Facebook has three API methods to help you. The facebook.fbml.refreshImgSrc method fetches and caches an image at a given URL. To refresh content from a given URL, you use the facebook.fbml.refreshRefUrl method. Lastly, to use content as a handle in FBML, you can call the facebook.fbml.setRefHandles method.

Feed

To update a user's news feed, the REST API has two methods. To publish information to an individual user's feed, the facebook.feed.publishStoryToUser method will publish information to a user's feed based on their session key (session_key) and their user ID (uid). You add the title, body, and various links, depending on what you want to publish. The second method, facebook.feed.publishActionOfUser, publishes a mini-feed story to the user's account, also based on their session key and user ID.

FQL

As I've mentioned, most of the calls in the REST API are wrappers for complex, but common, FQL queries. The `facebook.fql` method takes a query and returns a response object based on your syntax. In the Facebook documentation, most of the API requests have their FQL equivalents, so if you see you need something slightly different from what is provided in the API calls, check out the FQL equivalents before you start writing from scratch.

Friends

When you're developing applications, you might find it necessary to look at the friends of your users. There are three methods provided to deal with this. The method `facebook.friends.areFriends` will tell you whether two people are friends. The `facebook.friends.get` method returns a structure of the user's friends' user IDs. Lastly, the `facebook.friends.getAppUsers` method returns a structure of the friends of the user who have installed the application on which you're working.

Groups

If you want to work with your user's groups, the REST API has two methods that return information about their visible groups. When you call the `facebook.groups.get` method, you can retrieve all the groups the user belongs to, or a subset of these groups, by using the method's filtering mechanism. The second method, `facebook.groups.getMembers`, returns the user IDs (UIDs) for a given public group.

Marketplace

Facebook's marketplace is a place to buy/sell items, list jobs, list housing, or even request items to purchase/borrow through Facebook. You're able to search the Facebook marketplace with `facebook.marketplace.search`. There are getters and setters for listings with `facebook.marketplace.getListings` and `facebook.marketplace.createListing`. You can also remove listings with `facebook.marketplace.removeListing`. Facebook also has a category and a subcategory getter method, `facebook.marketplace.getCategories` and `facebook.marketplace.getSubCategories`.

Notifications

Facebook allows you to send and receive notifications in your application with the REST API. You can expose your user's request notifications, by using the `facebook.notifications.get` method, to see outstanding notification responses. You can also send notifications to your users with the `facebook.notifications.send` method and send invitations with the `facebook.notifications.sendRequest` method.

Photos

With more than 60 million images added each week by Facebook users, there are several REST methods to interact with users' images. You can tag images with the `facebook.photos.addTag` method or create photo albums with the `facebook.photos.createAlbum` method. You can get a user's individual photos with the `facebook.photos.get` method or a listing of their albums with the `facebook.photos.getAlbums` method. You can also get the listing of the tags that individual photos have with the `facebook.photo.getTags` method. I'll cover the workflow of this later, but you can also upload photos with the `facebook.photos.upload` method.

Profile

To easily interact with setting information in the user's profile, there are two methods to work with, `facebook.profile.setFBML` and `facebook.profile.getFBML`. I'll cover the FBML a bit later, but essentially these methods allow you to set and get FBML for a user's profile box and profile actions.

Users

The final set of methods in the REST API gives you access to some user information for your application. The first, `facebook.users.isAppAdded`, tells you whether the user has added your application. To get information from your user's profile, you can call the method `facebook.users.getInfo`. Lastly, to get the user ID (uid) from a session key, use the `facebook.users.getLoggedInUser` method.

Error Codes

Sometimes when you're developing an application, you make mistakes. Fortunately, Facebook returns rather robust error messages when something goes wrong (like you forgot to provide a specific parameter for an API call). The error codes are returned with both a numeric value and a message. Generally, if you receive an error message (in a structure), it's rather obvious when you read the error message (in the err_msg element). If you can't figure out what's going on with a specific call, it's always a good idea to check out the code in the API Test Console (http://developer.facebook.com/tools.php). Although this won't give you any more information than you are getting returned, it can help you narrow down what's going on (in case you have multiple errors).

Data Store API

Facebook also has implemented an API for basic database manipulations with its Data Store API (which is still in beta as of this writing). This API provides a basic create, read, update, and delete (CRUD) API for storing data that you access through REST. If you're unfamiliar with object-oriented database management systems (OODMSs), some of the terminology is a bit different from that for relational database management systems (RDBMSs). For instance, to use the Data Store API, you must define your *schema* (your database), which consists of object *types* (tables) and *properties* (columns).

One of the really nice features of the Facebook Data Store API is that Facebook does not plan to charge for normal use! You basically have use of Facebook's servers to perform your database manipulations for you. However, it's probably not quite time to get rid of your RDBMS yet, because there aren't any structured queries, full-text search, or transaction-level query processing in the Facebook Data Store API.

Note ➡ The Data Store API is still in beta as of the writing of this book. Because of this, there is a chance that what I write here will change. Please consult the wiki documentation for the latest information before you deploy any projects using the Data Store API.

The Data Store API consists of three basic functions: specialized tables, distributed tables, and associations that are split into five separate APIs (User Preference, Object Data Definition, Object Data Access, Association Data Definition, and Association Data Access). Since Facebook provides access to millions of users, the tables (objects) you create are distributed. Facebook does provide a specialized table of users that is optimized (if you find that you really need more, let the Facebook developers know at their Bugzilla site, http://bugs.developers.facebook.com/). The associations component of this API is a mechanism to provide performance for fast lookups (such as indexes). Because indexing tables in a distributed environment won't necessarily provide a performance boost, this mechanism has been implemented to provide fast lookups without centralized indexes or parallel queries.

The user preferences for the API consist of 128-character strings, for which you can store up to 201 for each user (numbered 0–200). Access to the getters/setters are accessed through getters and setters in the REST API (facebook.data.setUserPreference and facebook.data.getUserPreferences).

Data objects (that is, tables) are created with facebook.createObjectType. The object type takes a name and contains a set of object properties (that is, columns). Object properties have names and data types. You don't quite have the same type of control over the data types with the API as you do with your own RDBMS because you are limited to integers, strings (less than 256 characters), and text blobs (with a maximum of 64KB).

After defining your objects and object types, you create, read, update, and delete through the Object Data Access API. These are rather straightforward (facebook.data.createObject, and so on).

To work with the associations between objects, you first need to define the relationship between objects in the facebook.defineAssociation call. You can define two types of associations: one-way, symmetric associations and asymmetric associations. If you're familiar with RDBMS joins, think of an asymmetric association as a many-to-many join and a symmetric association as a one-to-many join. One-way associations are an association between objects that can happen only one way (in other words, there's no need to look up a value by some ID) for a given object. You then create the actual associations with the Association Data Access API. These methods allow you to create, remove, and retrieve these associations and retrieve the object details from the data contained in the data definition.

This can be confusing at first, so let's look at an example:

```php
<?php

$createObject = $facebook->api_client->data_createObjectType("wallpost");

$uid = $facebook->api_client->data_defineObjectProperty("wallpost", "uid", 1);

$time = $facebook->api_client->data_defineObjectProperty("wallpost", "timePosted", 2);

$post = $facebook->api_client->data_defineObjectProperty("wallpost", "post", 3);

?>
```

The previous snippet of code is analogous to the following SQL DDL:

```
CREATE TABLE wallpost(
```

```
    uid integer,
    timePosted timestamp,
    post text
)
```

As you can see in this simple example, this can take a little bit to get used to because you're not performing your typical SQL DDL; however, once you get your mind around how to create the objects, it's relatively trivial to use the API as the persistence layer for your application. I suspect that this API will eventually make it out of beta and be quite a powerful tool in the Facebook developer's toolbox, at least for those who choose to have Facebook manage their data.

FQL Primer

If you've worked with SQL before (and I assume you have), FQL isn't a big deal. You use the same syntax as typical ANSI-SQL, and there are only nine tables to deal with. There are, however, some important differences. There are no joins, and FQL has not implemented the LIMIT, GROUP BY, or ORDER BY clauses that are common to ANSI SQL–compliant implementations. Before we go any further, let's take a look at the tables and fields that are exposed to the Facebook Query Language.

Tables

Here's a list to make sure you know what's available to you in the different tables. (OK, these aren't really tables; more likely these are views of specific data, but for simplicity's sake, we'll just call them tables.)

- users(uid, first_name, last_name, name*, pic_small, pic_big, pic_square, pic, affiliations, profile_update_time, timezone, religion, birthday, sex, hometown_location, meeting_sex, meeting_for, relationship_status, significant_other_id, political, current_location, activities, interests, is_app_user, music, tv, movies, books, quotes, about_me, hs_info, education_history, work_history, notes_count, wall_count, status, has_added_app)

- friend(uid1, uid2)

- group(gid, name, nid, pic_small, pic_big, pic, description, group_type, group_subtype, recent_news, creator, update_time, office, website, venue)

- group_member(uid, gid, positions)

- event(eid, name, tagline, nid, pic_small, pic_big, pic, host, description, event_type, event_subtype, start_time, end_time, creator, update_time, location, venue)

- event_member(uid, eid, rsvp_status)

- photo(pid, aid, owner, src_small, src_big, src, link, caption, created)

- album(aid, cover_pid, owner, name, created, modified, description, location, size)

- photo_tag(pid, subject, xcoord, ycoord)

Functions and Operators

Although the FQL language isn't ANSI-SQL complete, it does have some simple operators and functions to help you work with user data. FQL has boolean operators (AND, OR, and NOT), comparison operators (=, >, >=, <, <=, <>), and arithmetic operators (+, -, *, and /). The functions included in FQL, although not exhaustive, allow you to perform some basic string manipulations. To conserve bandwidth, you can use the concat() function to group several tuples together:

```php
<?php

    $facebook_config['debug']      = false;
    $facebook_config['api_key']    = '<your_api_key>';
    $facebook_config['secret_key'] = '<your_secret_key>';

    require_once('<path_to_client_library>/facebook.php');

    $facebook = new Facebook($facebook_config['api_key'],
        $facebook_config['secret']);

/**
 * Ensure the user has logged on to Facebook
 */
    $user = $facebook->require_login();

/**
 * Construct the FQL request
 */
    $fql = "SELECT concat(first_name, ' ', last_name)
```

```
        FROM user
        WHERE uid =   '$user'";

/**
 * Pass the FQL to Facebook through the API client
 */
    $fql_result = $facebook->api_client->fql_query($fql);

/**
 * Print the results to the screen
 */
    echo "<pre>FQL Result:" . print_r($fql_result, true) . "</pre>";
?>
```

The previous example simply selects the first and last names of the user who is currently making the request. The resulting page will display an array in the following format:

```
FQL Result:Array
(
    [0] => Array
        (
            [anon] => <your_first_name> <your_last_name>
        )
)
```

You might be saying to yourself, "This is pretty useless. What's the difference between this and just calling both the fields?" Well, if you have any bandwidth concerns, you can alleviate some of those issues by using the concat function to put fields that you need together. For instance, you might want to put a specific string into your page that combines several fields in a specific way. Letting the Facebook servers do some of this processing before it gets back to your server will not only decrease your server load but can also cut down on your bandwidth in order to speed up your application.

Not only can you do simple SQL-style selects, but you can also perform subqueries. Take, for example, this FQL equivalent for the facebook.events.get REST API call:

```
SELECT eid, name, tagline, nid, pic, pic_big, pic_small, host, description,
        event_type, event_subtype, start_time, end_time, creator, update_time,
        location, venue
FROM event
WHERE eid IN (SELECT eid FROM event_member
                WHERE uid=uid AND rsvp_status=rsvp_status) AND
        eid IN (eids) AND
```

Graham

```
end_time >= start_time AND
start_time < end_time
```

I won't go into the theory behind nested queries, but I will mention that they are very useful for testing set membership, set comparisons, and set cardinality. And, this expansion of the REST call serves as a good example for writing your own custom FQL expressions.

You might find that you will need to take some additional processing to make sure your information is displayed in a specific order. You'll have to do this with your client language. For PHP, you need to sort the array and then slice it. Let's take the following:

```php
<?php
    $fql = "SELECT eid, name, location
        FROM event
        WHERE eid IN (
            SELECT eid
            FROM event_member
            WHERE uid = '$user'
        )";

    $fql_result = $facebook->api_client->fql_query($fql);

    asort($fql_result);

    array_slice($fql_result, 0, 5);

?>
```

The previous passes an FQL query to find events for the current user, sorts the resulting PHP array, and returns the array with the six elements (positions 0–5) of the query result.

FQL allows you as a developer to have granular control of the information that you retrieve about your users from the Facebook servers. Although it's not as robust as you might sometimes need (or want) it to be, you can generally get around FQL's limitations with some post-processing in the language in which you're developing. Additionally, as the complexity of your FQL increases with subqueries, you might at some point run into problems. As I've mentioned earlier, using the Facebook API Test Console at http://developer.facebook.com/tools.php is a great place to help debug your code. For instance, if you take the previous query and take out the WHERE clause so that your FQL statement reads as follows:

```
SELECT eid, name, location
    FROM event
    WHERE eid IN (
        SELECT eid
```

```
    FROM event_member
)
```

then, when executed, this will raise an error (shown in Figure 3-2) because you must have a limiting WHERE clause.

```
<?xml version="1.0" encoding="UTF-8"?>
<error_response xmlns="http://api.facebook.com/1.0/" xmlns:xsi="http://www.w3.org/2001/X
  <error_code>601</error_code>
  <error_msg>Parser error: WHERE clause is required.</error_msg>
  <request_args list="true">
    <arg>
      <key>query</key>
      <value>SELECT concat(first_name, ' ', last_name)
                FROM user

</value>
```

Figure 3-2. XML error response

If you missed it when you look at your code, the resulting XML response shows an error code of 601 and an error message of "Parser error: WHERE clause is required." Fortunately, this is an easy fix, but you might find yourself working with more complicated interactions with FBML and FQL, and this tool can provide invaluable help in discerning where your bugs exist.

Facebook Markup Language Primer

The Facebook Markup Language (FBML) is the heart of the Facebook platform. You might see some folks referring to FBML as "fancy" HTML tags, but it actually does a little more than static HTML because it has a dynamic connection to the Facebook back end. If you have developed any web applications in ColdFusion or JSP (using JSTL), programming with FBML will be very familiar. The Facebook Markup Language is described on the wiki site as an "evolved subset of HTML," so you have many of the same tags available to you as you do in normal HTML, but you also get a much richer tag set that allows you to code myriad interactions with the users very quickly.

Valid HTML Tags

For the most part, most commonly used HTML tags will work on the Facebook platform. If you've worked with HTML in the past, you're already familiar with this part of the platform. One major difference between typical HTML and FBML is that "normal"

JavaScript is stripped from your code. For instance, you cannot use the `onclick` attribute in the anchor (`<a>`) tag to call JavaScript:

```
<p>
    <a href="javascript:alert('You\'ll never see me');">click me</a>
</p>
```

Although completely valid HTML and JavaScript, the previous will raise an error (shown in Figure 3-3) when your users look at the page containing this code.

```
Errors while loading page from application
Runtime errors:

HTML error while rendering tag "a": Invalid scheme for url (javascript:alert('You\'ll never

There are still a few kinks Facebook and the makers of apress sample 1 are trying to iron out. We appreciate your patience as we
try to fix these issues. Your problem has been logged - if it persists, please come back in a few days. Thanks!
```

Figure 3-3. Facebook errors

Don't worry, if you need access to JavaScript for your application, Facebook has developed FBJS, which will allow you to use many of the conventions you typically see in JavaScript.

When working with FBML, remember that it's not exactly HTML, even though you use a lot of the same syntax. Your code has to be processed through the Facebook platform to ultimately generate the HTML that gets rendered to the user, so not everything you're used to doing with HTML code will work.

FBML Tags

FBML-specific tags are really the meat of the Facebook platform. The tag set isn't overly complex, but it has already gone through two iterations with FBML 1.0 and FBML 1.1. This change actually raises a sometimes-frustrating aspect in how Facebook changes the platform. When FBML 1.1 was announced in August 2007, developers basically had ten days to make their code compliant to the new specification. It is imperative that if you're developing an application for Facebook that you keep up with the changes to the platform so your application doesn't stop working. If you haven't already subscribed, add the Facebook News feed (`http://developers.facebook.com/news.php?blog=1`) to keep abreast of changes.

I'll also take a moment here to talk briefly about some of the issues, err, enhancements that you will see when using FBML. One of the big things you'll notice is that there are FBML tags that will act differently in different locations. As an example, you can use

Graham

iframes on canvas pages, but you cannot use the same iframe on the code in the profile box. There is also a queue of requested tags that are being considered for inclusion with the next FBML tag set iteration. Although not all of these tags will make it into the official language, it's interesting to see what the developer community is requesting to be included. You can view and add to these requests at
http://wiki.developers.facebook.com/index.php/Requested_FBML_Tags.

The developer's wiki for the Facebook platform groups the tags by their function. I believe this is perhaps the most useful way to work with the FBML because of the sheer volume of tags (almost 100 as of version 1.1). Also, because of this volume, some tags will necessarily have more information about them than others. If you find some of these descriptions and examples insufficient, please refer to the official documentation for the tags.

FBML tags are set apart from other HTML tags with the fb prefix and follow the format `<fb:tag_name>`.

Conditionals

FBML contains many conditional tests that can help you cut down on implementing this code in your application. At the heart of these conditionals is the `<fb:if>` tag:

```
<fb:if value="true">
    <p>Hi</p>
</fb:if>
```

At first glance, this isn't that useful because the value attribute will always be true. This is where your programming language comes into play. To actually make this do something useful, you need to be able to dynamically set this value. Let's write a short test to see whether the logged-in user has a user ID of 12345 and show a customized message:

```
<?php
    $user = $facebook->require_login();

    $test = false; // you may also use 1/0 for true/false

    if($user == 0000001){
        $test = 1;
    }
?>

<fb:if value="<?php echo($test)?>">
    <p>This is the secret message.</p>
    <fb:else>
```

Graham

```
     <p>No secret message for you!</p>
</fb:if>
```

This is a nonsense example, but it shows how you can you use the `<fb:if>`/`<fb:else>` construct to display custom messages to your users. You will find that through your application development process you will start constructing more complex `<fb:if>`/`<fb:else>` statements. Fortunately, the developers of the Facebook platform anticipated this and have a set of tags that will do many of the most common types of conditional checking.

As I stated earlier, Facebook tags act differently in different sections of the web pages. These conditional checks can occur only on the canvas page of your application:

- `<fb:is-in-network>` displays content if a UID is in the specified network.

- `<fb:if-can-see>` displays content if the logged-in user can view the specified content. This is often used to implement your own privacy features in your applications.

- `<fb:if-can-see-photo>` displays content if the user is logged on and has permissions to view the photo specified.

- `<fb:if-is-app-user>` displays content if the specified user has accepted the terms of service for the application.

- `<fb:if-is-friends-with-viewer>` displays content if the user specified is friends with the logged-in user.

- `<fb:if-is-group-member>` displays content if the user is a member of the specified group.

- `<fb:if-is-own-profile>` displays content if the viewer is the profile owner

- `<fb:if-is-user>` displays content if the viewer is one of the specified users.

- `<fb:if-user-has-added-app>` displays content if the specified user has added the application to their account.

Unfortunately, there isn't an FBML construct for else if logic. If you need to perform multiple conditional checks, you will need to properly nest your if statements. Alternatively, you can use the FBML's switch construct.

The FBML `<fb:switch>` tag acts a bit differently than many programming languages that implement the construct. In FBML, the `<fb:switch>` tag evaluates a set of FBML tags and returns the tag information from the first tag that returns something other than an empty string:

```
<fb:switch>
    <fb:user uid="0000001" />
    <fb:default>This is the default statement</fb:default>
</fb:switch>
```

This code will display the contents of the `<fb:default>` tag since there's no user with a UID of 0000001. You may at some point need something a bit more complex for your tests. You are able to nest `<fb:if>` and `<fb:switch>` statements within an `<fb:switch>` tag for these more advanced conditional analyses in your code:

```php
<?php
    $user = $facebook->require_login();

    $test = false;

    if($user == 0000001){
        // Boolean true = 1
        $test = 1;
    }
?>
```

```
<fb:switch>
    <fb:if value="<?php echo($test)?>">
        <fb:switch>
            <fb:profile-pic uid="<?php echo($user)?>" />
            <fb:default>Inner default</fb:default>
        </fb:switch>
    </fb:if>
    <fb:default>Outer Default</fb:default>
</fb:switch>
```

As you've probably noticed, there's no case statements with breaks that you normally see in other programming languages. If you're familiar with the switch statements having case and break statements, just think of each tag as a distinct case with no need for a break statement. There are times where this could require more complex nesting of statements, but if you find your conditional statements getting too complicated, it's probably a good idea to take a step back from what you're doing and see whether you can find an alternative method to perform the same check. Also, as a programming note, the switch statement essentially has a break after the first true statement in the switch statement. If you place the `<fb:default>` tag at the top of your code block (which will always return true), the rest of your switch statement will not get evaluated.

User/Group Information

Working with your user's and group's information is an important part of any Facebook application. You want to let your users easily interact with other users of your application, and there are some specific FBML tags to help with these interactions:

- `<fb:name>` returns the user's name for the uid passed to the tag. This function has a lot of customizable features to allow you to display the possessive of the user's name and additional logic to handle users who have protected their profiles. For example, the `<fb:name uid="$user" ifcantsee="Anonymous">` tag returns "Anonymous" if the user has chosen not to show their name in their profile.

- `<fb:grouplink>` returns the name and a link of the group ID passed to the tag.

- `<fb:user>` displays content to the specified user and no one else.

- `<fb:pronoun>` renders a pronoun for a specific user. This is a fun tag to use because it has several attributes that let you choose the different formats of the pronoun's use, including possessive, reflexive, and objective forms.

- `<fb:profile-pic>` renders a linked image of a user's profile picture. By default this is a 50-by-50-pixel image. This is good for "iconifying" your user's interactions.

Profile Specific

You might find that you need to provide different content depending on where your users are accessing the application from. Facebook provides the following tags for displaying content inside the user's profile box:

- `<fb:wide>` displays content only when the profile box is the wide column.

- `<fb:narrow>` displays the content only when the profile box is the narrow column.

- `<fb:profile-action>` builds a link on the user's profile under their photo. You'll use this in conjunction with setFBML to send information to the user's profile. As a note, there is a 30-character limit for the contents of this tag.

- `<fb:user-table>` renders a table of the users (specified by the `<fb:user-item>` tag) you have specified. This tag works only on a user's profile page (will not render on the canvas page).

- `<fb:user-item>` defines a user for use inside the `<fb:user-table>` tag.

- `<fb:subtitle>` defines a subtitle for the profile box.

Embedded Media

Rich media is one of the cornerstones of the modern Internet…just look at YouTube. If you find a need to use embedded media in your application for music, games, or other rich media, you can use several tags to do this. This is an area in which FBML diverges from HTML because it is missing an <embed> tag. However, you are still able to use this functionality through the following tags:

- <fb:iframe> inserts an iframe into your application to pull in external sources to your application. This tag cannot be used in the profile page.

- <fb:photo> renders a picture that is in the Facebook repository and the user has permission to view.

- <fb:mp3> adds a Flash-based MP3 player that controls the MP3 file specified. Remember, this has to be the absolute path to the file.

- <fb:swf> renders a Flash object on the page of the specified absolute path. On profile pages, the SWF file is rendered as an image and rendered directly on canvas pages.

- <fb:flv> renders a Flash-based player to stream FLV content. This tag will use only .flv extensions, not other formats such as AVI.

- <fb:silverlight> is basically the same as the <fb:swf> tag, but for Microsoft's Silverlight-based content.

Visibility on Profile

You might encounter instances in which you want to display specific content to your users depending on their profile status with your application. FBML allows you to distinguish between the application owner, users, application users (those who have granted full access to your application), and those who have added the application to their accounts.

- <fb:visible-to-owner> displays content if the user is the owner. As a side note, if the user isn't the owner, this displays whitespace.

- <fb:visible-to-user> displays content to the specified user.

- <fb:visible-to-app-users> displays content if the user has granted full permissions to the application.

- <fb:visible-to-added-app-users> displays content if the user has added the application to their account.

Graham

Tools

Tag-based languages such as ColdFusion and JSTL have many tags that build portions of your application for you. Similarly, FBML has a set of tags to help you build some very useful portions of your application:

- `<fb:comments>` generates code to add comments to an application. It takes care of posting and redrawing pages that are posted to for a given UID.

- `<fb:google-analytics>` adds the JavaScript to your application so you can use Google Analytics to track your application usage.

- `<fb:mobile>` displays content for mobile users (`http://m.facebook.com`). Content outside of these tags will be ignored for mobile users.

- `<fb:random>` randomly rotates certain parts of your application content (for quotes, pictures, or even advertising). This tag not only can randomly choose an element from within the tag (defined by the `<fb:random-option>` tag) but also can weight these options to appear more often (or less often) than other options.

Forms

Working with form information is important in developing any online application. FBML has some constructs to help with these common tasks.

- `<fb:request-form>` creates a form for sending requests. This is a great way to let your users send requests to add the application (when used with the `<fb:multi-friend-seletor>` tag). You cannot use this tag if you are using iframes.

- `<fb:request-form-submit>` creates a submit button for use with the `<fb:request-form>` tag.

- `<fb:multi-friend-input>` renders a multifriend input field like the one used in the message composer.

- `<fb:friend-selector>` renders an autocomplete input box of the user's friends.

- `<fb:submit>` creates a JavaScript submit button for your forms. This is generally used when you want to use an image instead of a submit button, such as `<fb:submit><img src="path/to/image" /></fb:submit>`.

Graham

Other

Here are some miscellaneous tags:

- `<fb:js-string>` allows you to define a string to reference in FBJS. You can set this anywhere in your code, and it is not displayed to the user. For example: `<fb:js-string var="foo">This is the rendered text</fb:js-string>`.

- `<fb:fbml>` allows you to define the specific version of FBML. Currently, the valid versions include 1.0 and 1.1.

- `<fb:fbmlversion>` displays the version of FBML that is currently being used.

- `<fb:redirect>` redirects the browser to another URL in your application.

- `<fb:ref>` allows you to define FBML that resides at a specific URL that you then call through the tag. This is generally used when you want to update a lot of profiles without publishing the data on a per-user basis.

- `<fb:share-button>` creates a share button with either URL information or specific metadata.

- `<fb:time>` renders a time in the user's time zone.

- `<fb:title>` sets the page's title tag.

Editor Display

To work with editing data, Facebook has derived a set of tags grouped in this section. The rendered form will display in two columns with the label on the left and an input field on the right. The one caveat to using the `<fb:editor>` tags to create forms is that you cannot use mock Ajax. If you want to be able to use mock Ajax, you will need to manually create your own form.

- `<fb:editor>` is the outermost tag used to create an editable form.

- `<fb:editor-button>` creates a button for your form.

- `<fb:editor-buttonset>` creates a container for one or more buttons.

- `<fb:editor-cancel>` creates a cancel button for the form.

- `<fb:editor-custom>` allows you to insert whatever code you want, as long as it's valid FBML.

- `<fb:editor-date>` creates two select boxes in the form for the month and day.

Graham

- `<fb:editor-divider>` adds a horizontal line divider to your form.
- `<fb:editor-month>` creates a select box populated with the months of the year.
- `<fb:editor-text>` creates an input box for your form.
- `<fb:editor-textarea>` creates a textarea box for your form.
- `<fb:editor-time>` creates select boxes for hours, minutes, and an a.m./p.m. indicator for your form.

As an example of this usage, consider the following.

```
<fb:editor action="." labelwidth="100">

    <fb:editor-text name="input" label="Editor Text" />

    <fb:editor-textarea name="textarea" label="Editor Text Area" />

    <fb:editor-custom label="Custom Select">
        <select name="select">
            <option value="editor-custom">Editor Custom Select</option>
        </select>
    </fb:editor-custom>

    <fb:editor-divider />

    <fb:editor-date name="date" label="Date" />

    <fb:editor-month name="month" label="Month" />

    <fb:editor-time name="time" label="Time"/>

    <fb:editor-buttonset>
        <fb:editor-button value="Add"/>
        <fb:editor-button value="Edit"/>
        <fb:editor-cancel />
    </fb:editor-buttonset>
</fb:editor>
```

Remember, the form the `<fb:editor>` tag produces uses the Post method. If you use the `<fb:editor>` tag, you will need to write some code on your server to then do something, but the purpose of this example was to show how to use these tags in conjunction with one another to create a form. In this case, the previous snippet will render as depicted in Figure 3-4.

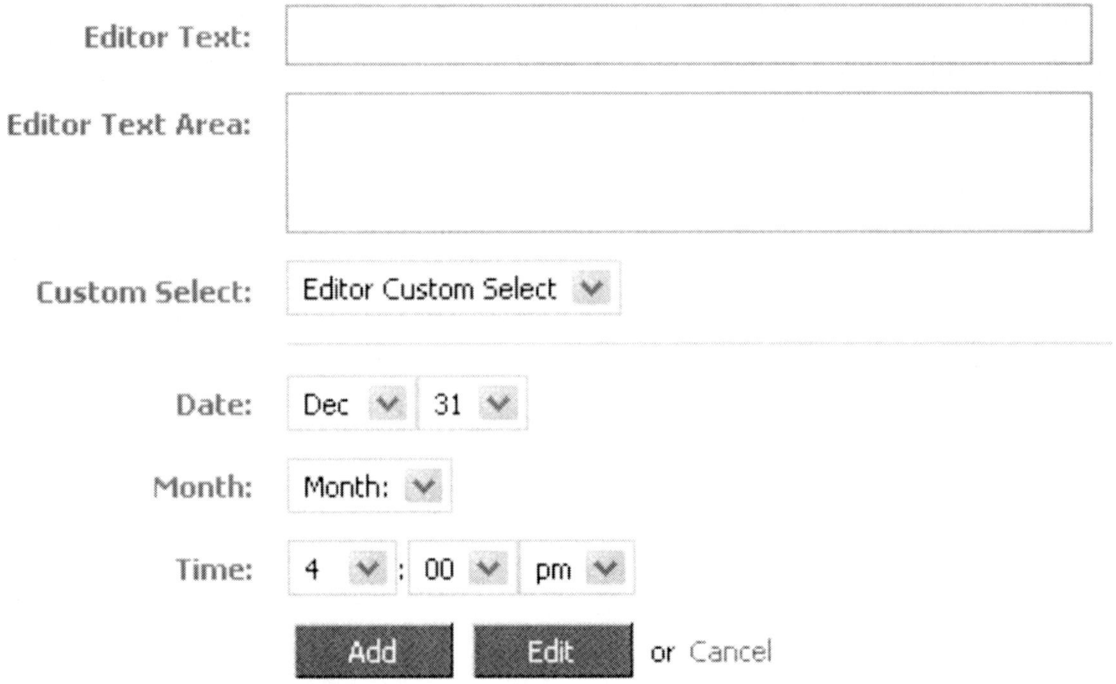

Editor Text:

Editor Text Area:

Custom Select: Editor Custom Select ▾

Date: Dec ▾   31 ▾

Month: Month: ▾

Time: 4 ▾ : 00 ▾   pm ▾

Add   Edit   or Cancel

Figure 3-4. Simple Facebook editor form

Page Navigation

Once you have your application completed, you're going to want to develop a navigation scheme for your users. The main tag for this task is the <fb:dashboard> tag that builds the familiar dashboard layout in Facebook. There are additional tags that you can lay out within the <fb:dashboard> tag, including buttons, hyperlinks, and even help:

- <fb:dashboard> renders the standard Facebook dashboard for navigation. This is a container tag for <fb:action>, <fb:help>, and <fb:create-button>. Note that you cannot use the <fb:if-user-has-added-app> tag inside this tag.

- <fb:action> is analogous to an anchor tag for the dashboard.

- <fb:help> creates a link to the application's help. This is rendered to the right side of the dashboard.

- <fb:create-button> creates a button for in the dashboard.

- `<fb:header>` renders a title header.

- `<fb:media-header>` renders a media header. This tag is generally used to display user-contributed content to specific users.

- `<fb:tabs>` is a container to add tabbed-navigation style of links to your application. Individual tab items are added with the `<fb:tab-item>` tag.

You can see the difference between how the tag sets for the dashboard (Figure 3-5) and tabs (Figure 3-6) generate content. The `<fb:dashboard>` tag allows you to nest `<fb:action>`, `<fb:help>`, and `<fb:create-button>` tags:

```
<fb:dashboard>
    <fb:action href=".">Add Something</fb:action>
    <fb:action href=".">Delete Something</fb:action>
    <fb:help href=".">Help me</fb:help>

    <fb:create-button href=".">Add Something</fb:create-button>
</fb:dashboard>
```

Figure 3-5. Facebook dashboard using `<fb:dashboard>` tags

The `<fb:tabs>` tag, by contrast, allows only the `<fb:tab>` tag to be nested:

```
<fb:tabs>
    <fb:tab_item href="." title="Add Something" />
    <fb:tab_item href="." title="Delete Something" />
    <fb:tab_item href="." title="Help Me" />
</fb:tabs>
```

Add Something	**Delete Something**	**Help Me**

Figure 3-6. Facebook tabs using `<fb:tabs>` tag

Both of these tag sets provide different functionality to you. Typically you will use <fb:tabs> for creating an overall navigation schema, and you will use <fb:dashboard> for performing functions within your application.

Dialog Boxes

As a note, this set of tags is still in beta mode, but basically this is a mechanism to provide modal dialog boxes for your application. This is really a fancy pop-up box to interact with your users. If this tag doesn't fit your needs, you can also use FBJS to create this type of interaction between your users by utilizing the Dialog object.

- <fb:dialog> is the container tag for the dialog box.

- <fb:dialog-title> is an optional title for your dialog box.

- <fb:dialog-content> is the message contained in the dialog box.

- <fb:dialog-button> renders a button for the dialog box.

Consider the following FBML snippet for constructing a dialog box:

```
<fb:dialog id="fb_test">

    <fb:dialog-title>This is a test</fb:dialog-title>

    <fb:dialog-content>Content</fb:dialog-content>

    <fb:dialog-button type="button" value="Okay" close_dialog="1" />

</fb:dialog>

<a href="" clicktoshowdialog="fb_test">show fb:dialog</a>
```

The <fb:dialog> snippet will render a modal window as shown in Figure 3-7. Within the <fb:dialog-content> tag, you are also able to add other information (and other FBML) tags, such as forms to perform more advanced interactions with your users.

Figure 3-7. FBML `<fb:dialog>`

For example, take this snippet that generates a search form to search Facebook (or some other site):

```
<fb:dialog id="fb_search" cancel_button="true">

    <fb:dialog-title>Search Facebook</fb:dialog-title>

    <fb:dialog-content>

        <form action="http://www.facebook.com/s.php" method="get">

            <input type="text" name="q" />

            <input type="submit" value="Search" />

        </form>

    </fb:dialog-content>

</fb:dialog>

<a href="" clicktoshowdialog="fb_search">Show Search</a>
```

Now, when the user clicks the Show Search link, a modal window will pop up, as shown by Figure 3-8. When users hit the Search button, they are passed to the new server, which in this case presents users with their search results.

Figure 3-8. `<fb:dialog>` *with form*

As mentioned previously, you can make these dialog boxes using FBJS (using the `Dialog` object). However, not everyone is a JavaScript expert, so the `<fb:dialog>` tags provide a convenient method to do most of the same things you can do with FBJS without writing any FBJS.

Wall

You might want to add the ability for your users to do something along the lines of your wall. There is functionality for this with the following:

- `<fb:wall>` renders a wall-like section in your application that has `<fb:wallpost>` elements from your application users.

- `<fb:wallpost>` is the message for the wall post that can contain an `<fb:wallpost-action>` element.

- `<fb:wallpost-action>` adds a link at the bottom of the wall post content. Even if you put it at the beginning of the `<fb:wallpost>` element, the display will still render at the bottom of that particular post.

Walls are pretty easy to implement, assuming you have some type of persistence mechanism (such as an RDBMS). Assuming you do have an RDBMS, you would simply make a new table with three tuples (columns) to hold the UID (bigint), the actual post (text), and a time stamp (for indexing). Additionally, you could add a primary key field, though the time stamp should suffice for this. Now, all you need to do is loop over these results to provide them in the `<fb:wallpost>` tags, and all this should be wrapped in `<fb:wall>`. The only hard part is deciding how many posts you want to display on a page.

Mock Ajax

If you've been working with online applications over the past several years, chances are you've at least heard of Ajax (asynchronous JavaScript and XML). This technology allows you to work with dynamic information from within a single page without needing to repost the data. The basic idea of how Facebook has implemented this is that you make a call to your callback URL (the code hosted on your server) and echo it back to the user.

You'll need to create a proxy file on your server to handle the responses from your mock Ajax. For our sample purposes, I'll show how to create a bit of code that allows users to type in text, and the Facebook platform will echo back the SHA1 hash of the string using mock Ajax. First, you need to create the Ajax proxy:

```php
<?php

/**
 * @title hashproxy.php
 */

    echo("Your encrypted text: " . sha1($_POST['q']));

?>
```

This file doesn't do anything really interesting; it just echoes back the string it's passed as an SHA1 hash. There's no special processing, but if you were using this to produce search results from, say, a database, you would process your results here.

Next, you need to add some FBML to a page to call the proxy. The FBML code to do this is pretty straightforward because it is similar to an HTML form. The only real difference is in the submit button that includes three additional FBML-specific attributes:

```html
<form id="hashForm">
    <label for="clearText">Text to hash:</label>
    <input type="text" name="clearText" />
    <input type="submit"
        value="Hash it"
        clickrewriteform="hashForm"
        clickrewriteid="hashResult"
        clickrewriteurl="<your_callback_domain>/hashproxy.php" />
</form>

<div id="hashResult"></div>
```

This bit of code will create a form on your application's page. When a user enters text into the input box and clicks the submit button, Facebook will take the results of the form (defined by the `clickrewriteform` attribute) and write the results from the `hashproxy.php` file (defined by the `clickrewriteurl` attribute) to the `hashResult` div (defined by the `clickrewriteid` attribute).

You can also include a loading indicator to help you let your users know that something is being processed. You just need to add a `clicktoshow` attribute that maps to a new element in the hashResult div:

```
<form id="hashForm">
    <label for="clearText">Text to hash:</label>
    <input type="text" name="clearText" />
    <input type="submit"
        value="Hash it"
        clickrewriteform="hashForm"
        clickrewriteid="hashResult"
        clickrewriteurl="<your_callback_domain>/hashproxy.php"
        clicktoshow="thumper" />
</form>

<div id="hashResult">
    <img src="<your_callback_domain>/loader.gif" id="thumper"
style="display:none;"/>
</div>
```

Note ➡ Need a loader? There are several really nice sites where you can grab these. One site that I like is Ajaxload (`http://www.ajaxload.info`), which allows you to set the foreground and background colors for a set of animated GIFs. Another nice site with a collection of loaders is at `http://www.napyfab.com/ajax-indicators/`. Just remember that using these indicators does add a little bit of overhead to your application because it has to start and stop the indicator when it gets its information. Depending on what you're doing, you might spend more time turning the image on and off than actually displaying the text, so doing a little testing to see whether having these load indicators helps with the design can go a long way in alleviating frustrations for your users.

You can also use mock Ajax from within anchor tags (`<a>`) with one small difference. You need some type of form to work with the mock Ajax, so you'll need to create an empty form:

```
<form id="dummyform"></form>

<a clickrewriteform="dummyform"
```

Graham

```
clickrewriteid="clickResults"
clickrewriteurl="<your_callback_domain>/response.php"
clicktoshow="thumper">click me</a>

<div id="clickResults"></div>
```

This type of interaction is very useful, and it will be able to handle most of the basic types of information retrieval you might need in your application. However, you might find that simply echoing results to the page falls a bit short of your needs. To develop more robust Facebook features that leverage JavaScript-style code, Facebook has developed the Facebook JavaScript language, which I'll cover next.

Facebook JavaScript Primer

As I stated earlier, Facebook will strip most JavaScript from your code because of security concerns. However, the Facebook developers realized that JavaScript is useful for developing enriched user interfaces. As a result, Facebook created its own version of JavaScript called Facebook JavaScript. However, I should note that FBJS is still currently in beta and subject to change.

If you've developed for other social web sites that allow you to use JavaScript, you know that they force you to use iframes in order to isolate their code. Facebook, however, takes a different tact for dealing with JavaScript. It takes its FBJS, parses the code, and prepends functions and variable names with your application identifier. For example, the following:

```
function say_hello(name){
    var my_string = 'this is a sample.';
    return my_string + ' ' + name;
}
```

is translated into this:

```
function <app_id>_say_hello(<app_id>_name){
    var <app_id>_my_string = 'this is a sample.';
    return <app_id>_my_string + <app_id>_name;
}
```

There are a few things to keep in mind when you are using FBJS in your applications. For instance, depending on the area your application resides in, your scripts will perform differently. Let's look at the following example from the Facebook wiki:

```
<a href="#" id="hello" onclick="hello_world(this); return false;">Hello World!</a>

<script>
<!--
function random_int(lo, hi) {
    return Math.floor((Math.random() * (hi - lo)) + lo);
}

function hello_world(obj) {
    var r = random_int(0, 255);
    var b = random_int(0, 255);
    var g = random_int(0, 255);
    var color = r+', '+g+', '+b;

    obj.setStyle('color', 'rgb('+color+')');
}

hello_world(document.getElementById('hello'));
//-->
</script>
```

This simple program randomly sets the color of the anchor text "Hello World"…nothing too special there. However, depending on where your application is located, it will behave differently. In the profile box, inline scripts like the previous are deferred until the first "active" event is triggered (for example, anything that requires a mouse click).

Note ➡ In early versions of FBJS, it was necessary to encapsulate the script code in HTML comments within the `<script>` tag. Facebook has since updated the code parsers to make this step unnecessary. And, as the platform becomes more sophisticated, other subtle changes like this should be expected.

DOM Objects

Part of Facebook's implementation of FBJS includes DOM objects. If you've worked with DOM before, FBJS typically prefixes the JavaScript equivalent with get and set. For instance, the JavaScript href object is called with getHref() and is set with setHref().

Putting It Together

Now that you have an idea of how all the different parts of the program work and a brief introduction to the "glue" that puts them together (the client libraries), it's worth taking a look at a basic example to illustrate how each of these components work together to show the platform at work.

This sample is a simple application that allows users to set their status using the PHP client library, the Facebook API, FQL, mock Ajax, and FBML. I'll show how to do this in a single file for the ease of the discussion (plus it's not that complicated).

If you haven't already done so, set up a new application because you'll need an API key and secret. You'll also need to set up your client libraries. If you need help with either of these, refer to Chapter 2.

The first step is to create a new page. If you have pointed your callback URL to `http://www.foobar.com/facebook`, you'll create a new `index.php` file in the `facebook` folder of your web root. In that page, you first need to set up a few variables:

```php
<?php

    $facebook_config['debug']      = false;
    $facebook_config['api_key']    = '<your_api_key>';
    $facebook_config['secret_key'] = '<your_secret_key>';

    require_once('<path_to_client_library>/facebook.php');

    $facebook = new Facebook($facebook_config['api_key'],
        $facebook_config['secret']);

    $user = $facebook->require_login();
?>
```

This simply sets up some constants (`api_key` and `secret_key`) and instantiates a `facebook` object (which includes an instance of the API REST client). You'll notice that this doesn't actually do anything, other than create a new `facebook` object and gets the user ID (UID), so let's add something to the page:

```html
<div style="padding:5px;">
    <h1>Hello
        <fb:name uid="<?= $user?>" firstnameonly="true" capitalize="true" />
    </h1>

    <p>What's your status?</p>
```

```
<form>
    <input type="text" name="status" value="confused" />
    <input type="submit"
        clickrewriteid="curr_status"
        clickrewriteurl="<your_callback_url>" />
</form>
<div id="curr_status"></div>
</div>
```

You'll notice that you use the user variable you set in the PHP code to display the user's name. You also set a mock Ajax call to populate the empty preview div. All that's needed now is to write some code to handle updating the status:

```
if(isset($_REQUEST['status']))
{
    // check permissions
    $has_permission =
        $facebook->api_client->call_method("facebook.users.hasAppPermission",
            array("ext_perm"=>"status_update"));

    if($has_permission){
        //update status
        $facebook->api_client->call_method("facebook.users.setStatus",
         array("status" => $_REQUEST['status']));

        // grab the status
        $fql = "SELECT status FROM user WHERE uid=" . $user;
        $query_result = $facebook->api_client->fql_query($fql);
        $status = $query_result[0]['status']['message'];

        echo("<p>Your status is now: <strong>" . $status . "</strong></p>");
    } else {
        $url = '<a href="http://www.facebook.com/authorize.php?api_key=';
        $url += $api_key . '&v=1.0&ext_perm=status_update">Click here</a>';

        echo('<p style="font-size:14px;"> ');
        echo('D\'oh...it doesn\'t look like you have permissions to change your
            status. ' . $url . ' to add the permissions to update your
            status.');
```

```php
    echo('</p>');

  }

  exit;
}
```

Because updating the user's status requires additional permissions, you're first checking the permissions for the user. If the user has permission, you update the status using an API call, and then you query Facebook with FQL to make sure that the status you just set is in fact the current status. Then you display it within the curr_status div.

When you put all these parts together, you get the following:

```php
<?php
/**
 * @title index.php
 * @description Simple status updater
 */

$facebook_config['debug']      = false;
$facebook_config['api_key']    = '<your_api_key>';
$facebook_config['secret_key'] = '<your_secret_key>';

require_once('<path_to_client_library>/facebook.php');

$facebook = new Facebook($facebook_config['api_key'],
    $facebook_config['secret']);

$user = $facebook->require_login();

if(isset($_REQUEST['status'])){

    // check permissions
    $has_permission = $facebook->api_client->call_method(
        "facebook.users.hasAppPermission",
        array("ext_perm"=>"status_update")
    );

    if($has_permission){
        //update status
        $facebook->api_client->call_method(
            "facebook.users.setStatus", array("status" => $_REQUEST['status'])
        );
```

Graham

```
        // grab the status
        $fql = "SELECT status FROM user WHERE uid=" . $user;
        $query_result = $facebook->api_client->fql_query($fql);
        $status = $query_result[0]['status']['message'];

        echo("<p>Your status is now: <strong>" . $status . "</strong></p>");
    }else {
        $url = '<a href="http://www.facebook.com/authorize.php?api_key=';
        $url += $api_key . '&v=1.0&ext_perm=status_update">Click here</a>';

        echo('<p style="font-size:14px;"> ');
        echo('D\'oh...it doesn\'t look like you have permissions to change your
            status. ' . $url . ' to add the permissions to update your
            status.');
        echo('</p>');
    }

    exit;
}
?>
<div style="padding:5px;">
    <h1>
        Hello
        <fb:name uid="<?= $user?>" firstnameonly="true" capitalize="true" />
    </h1>

    <p>What's your status?</p>

    <form>
        <input type="text" name="status" value="confused" />
        <input type="submit" clickrewriteid="curr_status"
            clickrewriteurl="<your_callback_url>" />
    </form>
    <div id="curr_status"></div>
</div>
```

This simple application shows several of the aspects I covered in this chapter in actual action.

Graham

Note ➡ The PHP client library includes a sample application named Footprints. This is a great application that shows how an entire Facebook application is put together.

Things to Remember

The Facebook platform has some quirks since the code you write is interpreted through Facebook. You might notice that when you create a form, Facebook creates several additional input fields in your form. These are used by Facebook to process your input but will be in there.

And, as another reminder, FBML isn't HTML! Although you can use many of the familiar tags in FBML as you have in HTML, there are differences in the way in which tags are processed. For instance, you might have noticed that there isn't a <link> tag in FBML. As you might have guessed, this limits your ability to use external CSS files for your application (Facebook also strips @import too). You have a couple of options to work around this limitation.

First, you can embed your CSS in the page using the <style> tag. Generally this isn't a big deal if you have a small application, but as your application grows, this becomes less manageable. A second method is to "fake" the style. Instead of using the <link> tag to point to your style file(s), you can create your style file as you normally would and include it within <style> tags in your PHP code. For instance:

```
<style>
    <?php require("style.css") ?>
</style>
```

This snippet will effectively include the style files for your application. You can also use the <fb:ref> tag to pull the entire style sheet (including the <style> tags). The best choice, of course, depends on your application, environment, and what you want to code.

If you look at the source for your generated page, you'll also notice that Facebook prepends your application key to the variables. For instance, if you define a style class of .foo, it, and every reference to this class, will be rewritten to .yourAppKey_foo.

Summary

This chapter covered the different parts of the Facebook platform. The main technologies in the platform consist of a REST API for data interchange, a language to querying information from Facebook's databases, and a language to render certain portions of the

Facebook platform to users (FBML). There are additional parts to the language that are more complex, such as Facebook JavaScript, and that are useful, but they're not a core part of the platform (that is, you don't need to use FBJS to develop your applications). The chapter also touched on the client libraries, which play an important part in gluing the Facebook platform to your development language. I also showed how to create a basic, functional application that updated the user's status message. To do this, you used an FBML form, mock Ajax, FQL, the PHP client library, and calls to the API.

In the next chapter, I'll kick things up a bit and show how to develop a more robust, complete application. I'll not only cover user interface design and development issues, but I'll also briefly discuss ways to monetize your application and where to go to find help when (or for you optimists, *should*) you get stuck. You'll use an RDBMS to keep track of user interactions, track usage with Google Analytics, and set up some useful libraries for code reuse.

CHAPTER 4

Building a Facebook Application, Start to Finish

By now you should have a good understanding of how Facebook allows you to implement your own code to extend its platform. I've covered how the different parts work, and I hope you've been able to take portions of the platform for a test-drive. However, I haven't talked about how all these pieces fit together. To that end, this chapter focuses on developing a Facebook application from start to finish.

For this example, I'll show how to develop a game review application. The application will allow users to rate games, write reviews, and interact with one another. Now, I'll preface this chapter with a notice that the driving force behind this application's design decisions is to show different aspects of the Facebook platform and may, at times, diverge from how you might ordinarily design and implement your own applications. Please keep in mind that there are multiple (and at times, better) ways to accomplish the same result, so if you see a better way to implement a specific element in the code examples, please, by all means, hack away.

You probably also have a favorite integrated development environment (IDE) that you use when developing your applications. I'll be using Eclipse as the IDE for this chapter because it provides a really great set of tools for developing in almost every language. Since Facebook Markup Language (FBML) is a superset of Hypertext Markup Language (HTML), the PHP Development Tools (PDT) plug-in will have most of the tags you will use (it just doesn't know about the Facebook-specific tags). I'll also show how to use some of the other Eclipse plug-ins to help you develop the database back end, as well as manage and test your code.

Setting Up Eclipse

IBM developed Eclipse as a Java IDE but soon open sourced the project and established the Eclipse Foundation, which hosts a growing number of extensible frameworks, tools, and runtimes in many different languages. And, with its multilanguage support, Eclipse provides a convenient platform when you're developing in multiple languages for a given project.

You can download the Eclipse IDE from http://www.eclipse.org/downloads/. The only other requirement to run this software is that you have a Java runtime installed on your system (JRE 5 is recommended, and JRE 1.4.2 is the minimum). If you need the latest Java Runtime Environment (JRE), you can download it from Sun at http://java.sun.com.

If you're not sure which version of Java you have installed, you can open a command prompt or terminal window and type the following:

```
java -version
```

You should see something along the lines of the following stating what JRE you have installed:

```
Java version "1.6.0_04"
Java(TM) SE Runtime Environment (build 1.6.0_04-b12)
Java HotSpot(TM) Client VM (build 1.6.0_04-b12, mixed mode, sharing)
```

If your JRE version is less than 1.4.2, you'll need a new version.

The download page for Eclipse displays several options for the different packages available. For the purposes of this book, you just want the latest Eclipse Classic package for your operating system. Once you've downloaded the software, simply unzip/untar the file to a convenient location (such as C:\eclipse or /opt/eclipse). To start the Eclipse IDE, launch the eclipse executable in the eclipse folder.

Note ➡ At the time of this writing, the most recent version of Eclipse is Europa (3.3). You may be running Eclipse 3.4 (Ganymede) or some other future version of Eclipse. Just replace mentions of *Europa* with whatever the name of the instance of Eclipse is that you're running.

When you launch the IDE, you will be prompted for the location where you want to set up your workspace. You can accept the default, or you can change this to a more convenient location.

Now out of the box, the IDE isn't that useful because, as mentioned, IBM originally developed this as a Java IDE. You'll need to add a couple of extensions before you can start developing. The first plug-in to add is the Remote System Explorer End-User Runtime extension from Eclipse. This plug-in will allow you to connect to your remote system to make edits (it supports SSH/SFTP, FTP, Local, Telnet, and Unix and Windows shares). I'll explain how to install it in the following sections.

Graham

Using Plug-Ins

One of the most powerful aspects of Eclipse is its extensibility through plug-ins. You'll use several of the official plug-in projects supported by the Eclipse Foundation to add the ability to connect to your remote site, have PHP syntax highlighting, and connect to your database instance. I'm sticking to the plug-ins developed as part of the Eclipse project, but there are a lot of other plug-ins that may fit your development cycle better. A good place to look for these plug-ins is the Eclipse Plugin Central web site at `http://www.eclipseplugincentral.com/`.

Remote Project Support (FTP/SFTP)

Eclipse recently repackaged its set of plug-ins to allow remote access to different file systems in one Remote System Explorer End-User Runtime plug-in. To install this plug-in, use the Europa Discovery Site (a project software repository for Eclipse) by clicking Help > Software Updates > Find and Install, as shown in Figure 4-1. Select the Search for New Features to Install in the Feature Updates Wizard, and click Next. Click the Europa Discovery Site check box to search, and click the Finish button. If you haven't selected the option to automatically select a mirror, you will be prompted to manually select a mirror (make sure you pick one that's close to you).

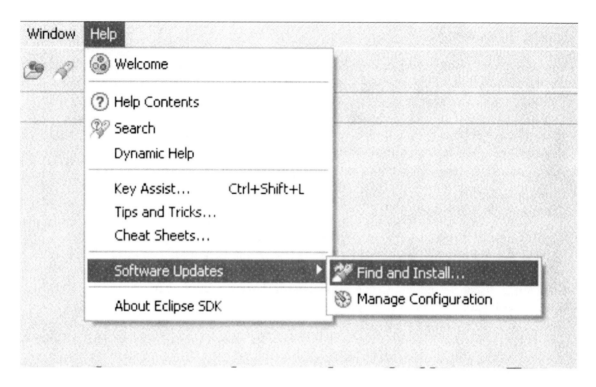

Figure 4-1. Eclipse updates

Once the mirror has been scanned for the software, expand the Europa Discovery Site, scroll down and expand the Remote Access and Device Development option, and select Remote System Explorer End-User Runtime. Then click Next. On the Feature License screen, select the option to accept the license, and click Next. You should have only one feature to install, on the next screen, and now click Finish to begin the installation (Figure 4-2).

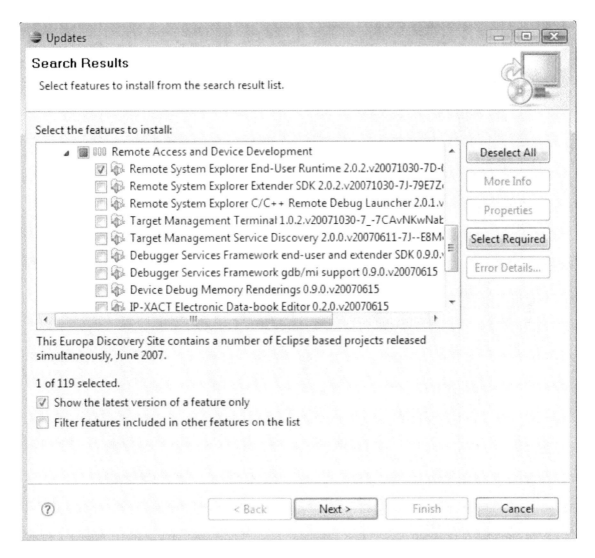

Figure 4-2. Installing the Remote System Explorer End-User Runtime plug-in

Once the plug-in has been downloaded, Eclipse will prompt you to restart the IDE. Go ahead and restart because it takes only a moment.

PHP Development Tools

The next plug-in you'll install is the PDT plug-in from Eclipse. However, Eclipse doesn't include this tool in its default listing, so you have to add it to the list of repositories. To start, you again select Help > Software Updates > Find and Install, making sure the Search for New Features to Install option is selected. Then click Next.

Click the New Remote Site button, name the update site PDT, enter the URL of `http://download.eclipse.org/tools/pdt/updates/`, and click OK (Figure 4-3).

Figure 4-3. Eclipse PDT update

Make sure the update site PDT and the Europa Discovery Site are selected, and click Finish. After you select the mirror, expand the tree PDT > PDT Features, and select PDT Features (see Figure 4-4). You'll notice that there's an error message at the top of the page letting you know that there are required features that you need to install. Expand the Europa Discovery Site > Web and JEE Development branch, and select the Web Standard Tools (WST) Project option. There are still unsatisfied dependencies, so now click the Select Required button, which will then select any additional packages that need to be downloaded.

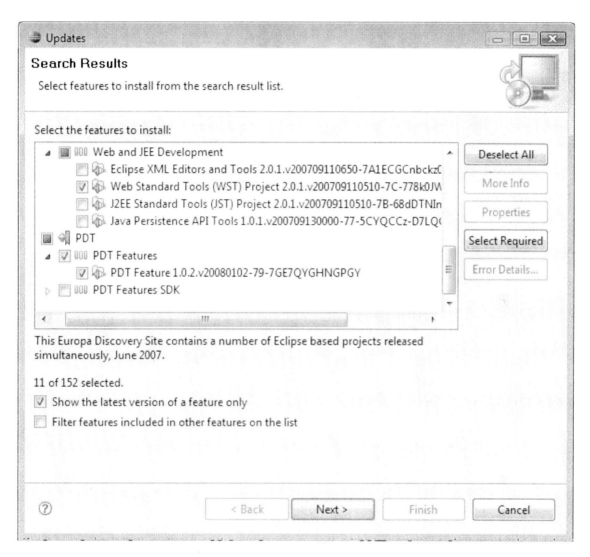

Figure 4-4. Eclipse feature installation

Click Next to view the individual licenses for each of the packages you need to download. After you've read them (you did read them, right?), accept the license agreement, and click Next. Then click Finish. After the software is finished installing, restart Eclipse.

Note ➡ PHPEclipse (`http://www.phpeclipse.de`) is another popular extension. It allows you to control Apache and MySQL from within Eclipse, which can save you some time. Joomlatwork (`http://www.joomlatwork.com`) has also developed an Eclipse package (to save you all the installation headaches) that you can download called PHP Development Studio. There's a free version as well as a paid version that includes some optimizations.

You can edit the setting for PDT by selecting Window > Preferences and expanding the PHP branch. It's worth looking at all the settings you can set to be familiar with them should you want to change anything in the future.

Data Tools Platform SQL Development Tools

Lastly, you'll install a SQL editor, along with some tools to ease working with your database back end. These tools are packaged in the Database Development branch of the Europa Discovery Site. Although you may already have a favorite tool for interacting with your relational database management system, the fact that Eclipse has an integrated tool for working with your data can be a boon to development.

As before, open the Europa Discovery Site in the updater. Then select the entire Database Development tree from the options, and click the Select Required button to satisfy the dependencies, as shown in Figure 4-5.

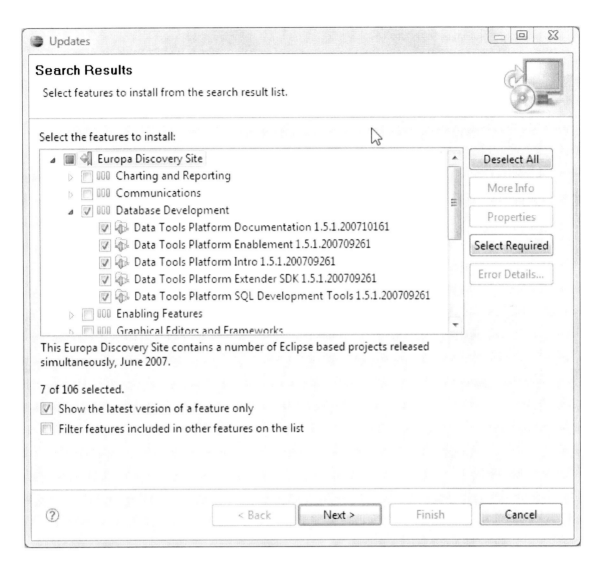

Figure 4-5. Data Tools Platform plug-in installation

After you've installed the plug-in and restarted Eclipse, the last thing to do is get the JDBC driver for your particular database back end. The examples in this book are using MySQL, so you can head over to the MySQL Connector/J web site (http://www.mysql.com/products/connector/j/) to download the latest driver. After saving the tarball to your hard drive, extract it to a convenient location:

```
tar zxvf mysql-connector-java-5.1.X.tar.gz
```

```
tar zxvf mysql-connector-java-5.1.X.tar.gz
mv mysql-connector-java-5.1.X/mysql-connector-java-5.1.X-bin.jar ~/java/jdbc/mysql
```

The previous example places the JDBC driver for MySQL in the current user's java/jdbc/mysql directory. If you're a Windows user, this is equivalent to C:\Documents and Settings\<user_name>\java\jdbc\mysql or C:\Users\<user_name>\java\jdbc\mysql. Wherever you decide to put these files, remember where they are!

The only remaining task is to tell Eclipse where the driver is. Open Eclipse's preferences (in the Window option of the taskbar), expand the Connectivity branch, and click Driver Definitions. From there, scroll down to the MySQL Section, click 5.1, and click Add (see Figure 4-6).

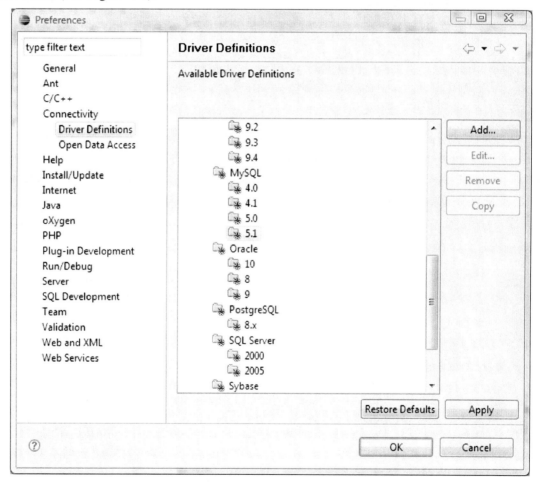

Figure 4-6. Adding the JDBC driver

Graham

Expand the Driver Template tree until you get the MySQL JDBC Driver template (Figure 4-7), and click OK.

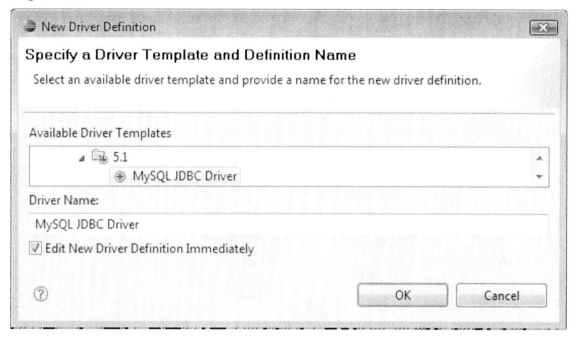

Figure 4-7. New driver definition

You will notice that Eclipse knows to look for the `mysql-connector-java-5.1.X-bin.jar` file you extracted earlier but doesn't have the path to the actual file. You correct this by clicking the driver file and clicking the Edit Jar/Zip option on the right. Just navigate to where you extracted your MySQL JDBC driver to, and click Open. This will clear the error for connecting to MySQL 5.1 database servers, so you can finish up by clicking OK until the dialog boxes are all closed.

To test your connection, change to the Database Development Perspective (Window > Open Perspective > Other). In the dialog box, select Database Development, and click OK.

From the wizard in the left toolbar (Figure 4-8), click the New Connection Profile icon, select Generic JDBC Connection, and click Next. Give a name and description for your connection, and select whether to establish the connection when Eclipse starts. This will cause Eclipse to take slightly longer to start up, or you can just establish the connection when you need it.

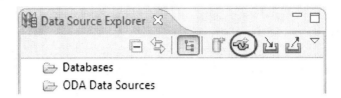

Figure 4-8. Adding a new database connection

In the New JDBC Connection Profile Wizard, select MySQL JDBC Driver from the drop-down list. This autopopulates most of the fields; all you need to do is edit them to match your environment (see Figure 4-9).

Figure 4-9. New JDBC connection profile

Assuming everything went well and there weren't any errors, you now have direct access to the data on the server. You can create a new SQL file for any defined projects in Eclipse by selecting File > New > SQL File (if you don't see it, select File > New > Other, expand SQL Development, select SQL File, and then click Next).

Note ➡ If you're working with a hosted database, make sure that the database server will accept outside connections. If not, you may need to edit your configuration files to include the IP address of the location from which you are working. Another alternative is to set up a local database that you can work with and then dump your SQL to your production server.

In the Create SQL File Wizard, give your file a name, select the database server type of MySQL_5.1, and select your newly created connection profile and database name. Once your connection is established, you can test your code by writing it, right-clicking the contents of the file, and selecting Execute All. You can also execute selected text by first selecting the portion of the SQL statement to execute, right-clicking, and selecting Execute Selected Text.

Connecting to Your Web Server

Now that the IDE is properly set up, let's set up the connection to your remote site. To do this, you'll change the perspective to the Remote System Explorer by selecting Window > Open Perspective > Other and selecting Remote System Explorer.

As part of a hypothetical sever configuration, let's say that your domain (www.foobar.com) is set up for FTP access. To set up access, click the Define a Connection to Remote System button at the top of the Remote Systems toolbar on the left (see Figure 4-10).

Graham

Figure 4-10. Adding an FTP connection

This will launch a wizard for you to add your site definition. Once you have completed the wizard, you can then connect to your web site by right-clicking the site definition and selecting Connect. This will give you live access to the files on your server to develop and edit your files as needed.

Layout Out the Project

For the purposes of this chapter, I'll show how to lay out your files in a rather simple manner, with each page serving a single purpose. You'll also create a layout to separate the files that you don't write into a separate folder. Since you're using the Remote System Explorer, you'll use this plug-in to help you set up the project in Eclipse.

You first need to set up an Eclipse project using the Remote System Explorer. This is a simple task, but it's not immediately evident if you've never done it before. Essentially, once you've created a connection to a remote resource, find the root folder you want to use as your project by expanding the directory listing in the left toolbar (shown earlier in Figure 4-10). Right-click the folder, and click Create Remote Project (Figure 4-11). This will set up a new project that you'll be able to see in the Package Explorer, and it will simplify a lot of tasks.

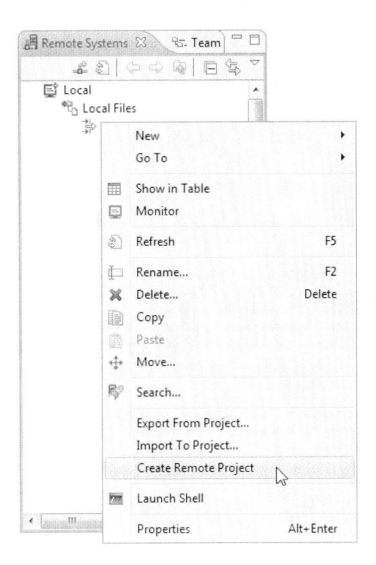

Figure 4-11. Creating a remote project

Before you go any further, let's change views to the PHP editor. Simply click the Open Perspective button (Figure 4-12) in the upper-right corner, select Other, and then choose PHP.

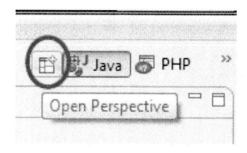

Figure 4-12. Changing the Eclipse perspective

This will change the perspective to the PHP editor from the PDT project. There's not much to look at right now, but I'll go through some of the features after you get a bit further in your setup.

The next step is to create some folder structure. You want to get the Facebook client library files in a lib folder under the root. First, you need to download the most recent version of the files. They're available for download at http://developer.facebook.com/resources.php. And, if you have wget (for example, you're not using Windows), you can download the client library with the following:

```
wget http://developers.facebook.com/clientlibs/facebook-platform.tar.gz
tar zxvf facebook-platform.tar.gz
```

After you've extracted the files, you need to get them into the project. First, create a folder under the root by right-clicking the root folder in Eclipse and selecting New > Folder. Then just type **lib**, and click Finish. Now select the newly created folder, right-click, and select Import. Expand the General tree, select File System, and click Next (Figure 4-13).

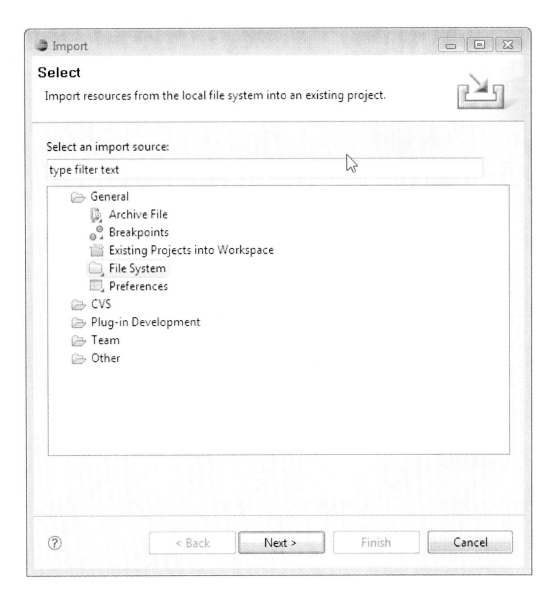

Figure 4-13. Using the Import Wizard

Now, navigate to where you extracted the client library, and click OK. Select the files facebook_desktop.php, facebook.php, and facebookapi_php5_restlib.php, and click Finish (see Figure 4-14).

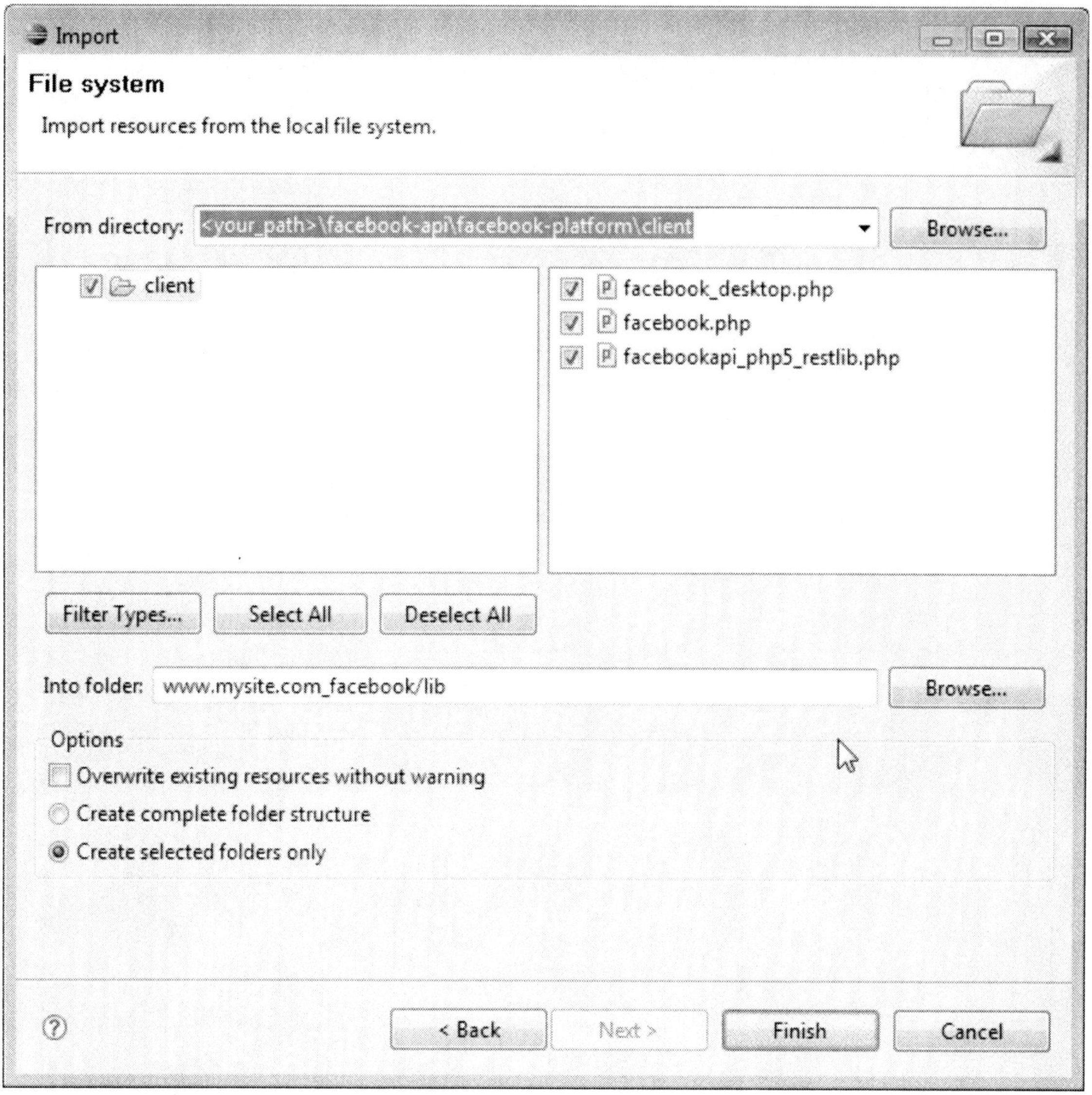

Figure 4-14. Importing Facebook client libraries

Next, for convenience, let's set up a file that you can include on your pages with some of the information you'll be using throughout the application. You'll create another folder called `config` and create a new file named `config.inc.php`. So, create the folder as you did before; then create a new file by right-clicking the `config` folder and selecting New PHP

File. Name the file config.inc.php, and click Next. Choose New Simple PHP File as the template, and click Finish.

Note ➡ If you don't see the option to create a new PHP file when you right-click a folder, make sure you are in the PHP perspective.

In your new file, let's include some code. The two most important pieces of information you'll need on every page is the API key and secret for your application. In case you didn't write them down when you applied for your application key, you can get to them in the Developer application by clicking My Applications in the top right.

So, let's add some code to your page. Using the code Facebook provides developers as a template, you'll set up your main include configuration as follows:

```php
<?php
/**
 *
 * File: config.inc.php
 *      This is the configuration file for the application
 *
 */

/*********************** Facebook Configuration ***********************/

// define the debug level (true|false)
$facebook_config['debug'] = true;

// define your API Key and secret
$facebook_config['api_key'] = '<your_api_key>';
$facebook_config['secret'] = '<your_secret>';

// include the facebook client library
require_once = '<path_to_libraries>/facebook.php';

// create the facebook object
$facebook = new Facebook($facebook_config['api_key'], $facebook_config['secret']);

// require users to be logged in
$user = $facebook->require_login();

// define your callback URL
```

```
$callback_url = '<your_callback_url>';

?>
```

Note ➡ So, what's the deal with the `.inc.` in the file name? Something you don't want to happen is for some of this information to be available to the Internet. To make sure these files are secure, it's a good idea to block these with `.htaccess` with a snippet like this:

```
<Files *.inc.php>
Order deny,allow
Deny from all
Allow from localhost
</Files>
```

In this code, you'll notice at the top of the file that you set the debug level to `true`. This is helpful while you're developing your application, but make sure you set this to `false` once you get ready to deploy your application!

Next I'll show how to set up a page with some visual aspects for your application. It won't be anything fancy, just a page that you can use to actually see something when you go to Facebook. You'll create a new index file in the root. However, before you do this, I'll take a second to show how to edit PHP templates to include some of your specific needs when developing your applications.

To edit the templates, click Window > Preferences. Then expand the PHP tree, and select Templates (see Figure 4-15).

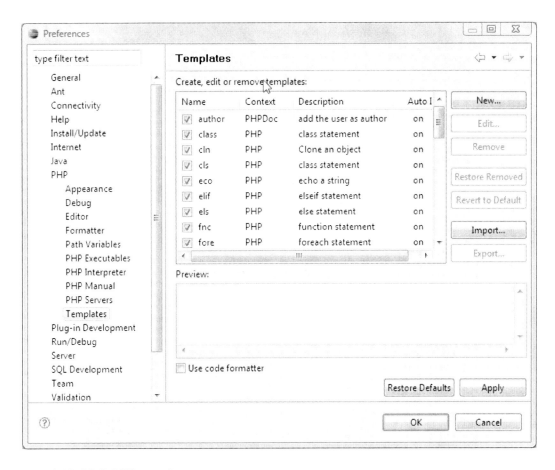

Figure 4-15. PDT PHP templates

To add a new template, click the New button in the upper-right corner. Name this new template New Facebook PHP, and change Context to New PHP. A description isn't necessary, but add the following in the Pattern area (see Figure 4-16):

```php
<?php
/**
 * File:
 * Description:
 */

require_once('config/config.inc.php');

?>
```

Click OK and then OK again when done.

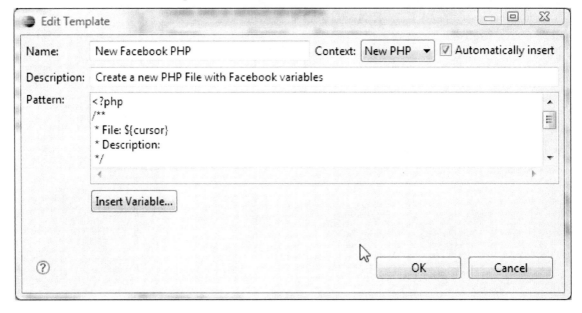

Figure 4-16. PHP template

Now when you create new pages for your application, this information will automatically be added. With that small task out of the way, let's make your first page.

Create a new PHP file by right-clicking the root folder and selecting New > PHP File. Name the file index.php, and click Next (not Finish). On the next screen, select the newly created new Facebook PHP file, and then click Finish. You now have a skeleton file for your application.

Next, you just need to fill in something on the page to make it actually have a display. For this, you'll use some FBML to display a success message to yourself to make sure everything is working. Add the following to the following to your page (below the PHP):

```
<fb:success
    message="Congratulations! Your first application is up and running..." />
```

If you take a look at your application now (you remembered to save it, right?) by navigating to http://apps.facebook.com/<your_app_name>, you should first be prompted to add the application, and then you will see the screen shown in Figure 4-17 in the main page of your application.

Figure 4-17. FBML success

Before you get too far into the UI design, let's take a step back and do a little planning for your database back end.

Creating the Database

When developing a web application, one of the more complex tasks is developing a database back end. For the purposes of this example, I'll be using MySQL since it's quite typical for developers to have this as their back end. If you're using another RDBMS such as PostgreSQL, Oracle, Derby, or Microsoft SQL Server, there won't be much of a difference because you won't be getting into any of the more advanced features of the RDBMS engine.

Designing the Database

Now that you have things set up, let's think about the design of your database. Like I mentioned at the beginning of the chapter, this is a game review system. It will show off how to do a bunch of techniques in Facebook to give you a good idea of how to use these features in your own application.

To begin your design, you'll need a table that holds review data. This table will hold a user ID (UID), the game being reviewed, a rating, and a generated primary key for convenience. You also need a game table to link to the review table that includes a game title, publisher, ESRB rating, game genre, and release year.

If you were developing this from scratch, you would use another table to record usernames, e-mail addresses, passwords (with some type of obfuscation in place), and other information such as names, addresses, and so on. Since Facebook takes care of all of this, the only information you really need from the user is the uid token in fields that will need any type of personal information for users. Just to reiterate, it's a good idea to keep as little personal information about your users as needed and use Facebook methods to return the information needed (such as usernames, where they're at, and so on) instead of storing these yourself. First, you could run afoul of Facebook's terms of use, but more than that, you waste development cycles implementing things that have already been developed.

Graham

For a more formal view of your database at this point, take a look at it in the entity relationship (ER) model shown in Figure 4-18.

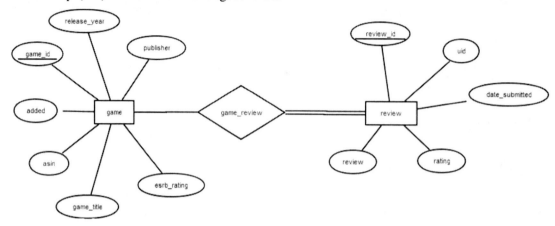

Figure 4-18. First game review ER diagram

ER diagrams provide a nice visual for your design to help you walk through some of the complexities of your design. Now that you have defined a couple of tables and a relation (the diamond), let's translate that into Data Definition Language (DDL) for MySQL. Figure 4-18 will translate into a slightly different table structure than I described earlier.

To create the table for games, you get the following:

```
CREATE TABLE game (
    game_id INTEGER UNSIGNED NOT NULL AUTO_INCREMENT,
    game_title VARCHAR(255) NOT NULL,
    esrb_rating VARCHAR(45) NOT NULL,
    release_year INTEGER UNSIGNED NOT NULL,
    publisher VARCHAR(45) NOT NULL,
    added TIMESTAMP DEFAULT CURRENT_TIMESTAMP NOT NULL,
    asin CHAR(10) DEFAULT '' NOT NULL,
    PRIMARY KEY (game_id)
);
```

And here's the table for reviews:

```
CREATE TABLE review (
    review_id INTEGER UNSIGNED NOT NULL AUTO_INCREMENT,
    uid BIGINT UNSIGNED NOT NULL,
    rating TINYINT UNSIGNED NOT NULL,
    review TEXT,
    game_id INTEGER UNSIGNED NOT NULL,
```

```
    date_submitted TIMESTAMP DEFAULT CURRENT_TIMESTAMP NOT NULL,
    PRIMARY KEY (review_id),
    FOREIGN KEY (game_id) REFERENCES game (game_id)
);
```

To take care of the game_review relation, I added the review_id tuple (column or field) to relate the game records to individual reviews. The timestamp tuples (added and date_submitted) will be used to display the most recently added games and reviews somewhere on your application. There's also a foreign key constraint on the review table since you don't want reviews for nonexistent games!

Working with SQL

Let's commit your DDL to your database now. Since you've already installed the DPT plug-in, all you have to do is launch the previous script in the SQL editor. You'll create a new SQL file with a connection to your database to insert the data. You'll also include some default data, just for testing purposes.

To add the new SQL file, switch to the Database Development view and select New > SQL File, or select New > Other > SQL Development > SQL File. Give your file a name (such as facebook_app), and set your connection information that you set up earlier (the database server type is MySql_5.1, the connection profile name is your connection profile, and the database name is your database name). Then click Finish.

Next, simply type the earlier code (or copy and paste it) into the file, and save it. To add the tables, add Go between the SQL statements, right-click, and select Execute All. Check with your favorite tool to see whether the tables were created properly.

It's time for some dummy data so you can have something in the database. For your games, you'll use some of the best games of all time. You can either create a new file or just paste these lines into the SQL file you've already created:

```
INSERT INTO game(game_title, esrb_rating, release_year, publisher)
VALUES("Super Mario Brothers","not rated",1995,"Nintendo");

INSERT INTO game(game_title, esrb_rating, release_year, publisher)
VALUES("Resident Evil 4","M",2005,"Capcom");

INSERT INTO game(game_title, esrb_rating, release_year, publisher)
VALUES("Final Fantasy III","E10+",1994,"Square");

INSERT INTO game2(game_title, esrb_rating, release_year, publisher)
VALUES("The Legend of Zelda: A Link to the Past","E",1992,"Nintendo");
```

```
INSERT INTO game(game_title, esrb_rating, release_year, publisher)
VALUES("Super Metroid","E",1994,"Ninetendo");

INSERT INTO game(game_title, esrb_rating, release_year, publisher)
VALUES("Half-Life 2","M",2004,"Vivendi Games");

INSERT INTO game(game_title, esrb_rating, release_year, publisher)
VALUES("Super Mario 64","E",1996,"Nintendo");

INSERT INTO game(game_title, esrb_rating, release_year, publisher)
VALUES("The Legend of Zelda: Ocarina of Time","E",1998,"Nintendo");

INSERT INTO game(game_title, esrb_rating, release_year, publisher)
VALUES("Civilization II","E",1996,"Microprose");

INSERT INTO game(game_title, esrb_rating, release_year, publisher)
VALUES("Tetris","E",1989,"Nintendo");

INSERT INTO game(game_title, esrb_rating, release_year, publisher)
VALUES("Halo 3","M",2007,"Microsoft/Bungee");
```

And here's some data for the reviews (you can change 7608007 to your own uid):

```
INSERT INTO review(uid, rating, game_id, review)
VALUES (7608007, 5, 1, 'I grew up on this game!!!');

INSERT INTO review(uid, rating, game_id, review)
VALUES (7608007, 4, 1, 'This game made me drop out of school!');

INSERT INTO review(uid, rating, game_id, review)
VALUES (7608007, 1, 1, "I wasn't even born when this came out!");

INSERT INTO review(uid, rating, game_id, review)
VALUES (7608007, 4, 2, 'Great game play');

INSERT INTO review(uid, rating, game_id, review)
VALUES (7608007, 3, 3, 'Team fighting is fun!');

INSERT INTO review(uid, rating, game_id, review)
VALUES (7608007, 4, 4, 'Save Hyrule from Gannon');

INSERT INTO review(uid, rating, game_id, review)
VALUES (7608007, 5, 5, 'Spoiler...Samus is a girl!');
```

Graham

```
INSERT INTO review(uid, rating, game_id, review)
VALUES (7608007, 5, 6, "Gordon just can't seem to catch a break.");

INSERT INTO review(uid, rating, game_id, review)
VALUES (7608007, 5, 7, 'First Mario Brothers in 3D
    -- can you get the rabbits outside the castle?');

INSERT INTO review(uid, rating, game_id, review)
VALUES (7608007, 5, 8, 'Gannon is back!');

INSERT INTO review(uid, rating, game_id, review)
VALUES (7608007, 1, 9, 'I blame Sid Meier for my F in Calculus');

INSERT INTO review(uid, rating, game_id, review)
VALUES (7608007, 1, 10, 'Simple puzzle...hours-o-fun!');

INSERT INTO review(uid, rating, game_id, review)
VALUES (7608007, 1, 11, 'Crush the Flood!');
```

Now you have some data in your database that you can play with. If you query the data (with SELECT * FROM game;), you will be able to see the games you just inserted (likewise for the review table).

Jumping In

I'm a fan of iterative development, and since you have a table structure and an application set up, in this section you'll get the application to do something. For this iteration, you'll add some basic functionality such as the ability to view, add, and publish game reviews. For your initial view, you'll develop a page that will list recently reviewed games and have a logical navigation to add reviews and ratings.

For your index page, you'll set up some CSS for your entire site and some basic FBML for interacting with users. For your style sheet, you'll use a trick to include the style file with a require_once statement. You'll also set up some basic CSS styles to hold different boxes to hold content areas. You need to make your style sheet file for your site in a folder named style.

The WTP plug-in you installed when you added the PDT plug-in includes a CSS editor, so to create a new CSS file, you simply right-click in the navigation panel, and select New > CSS (see Figure 4-19).

Graham

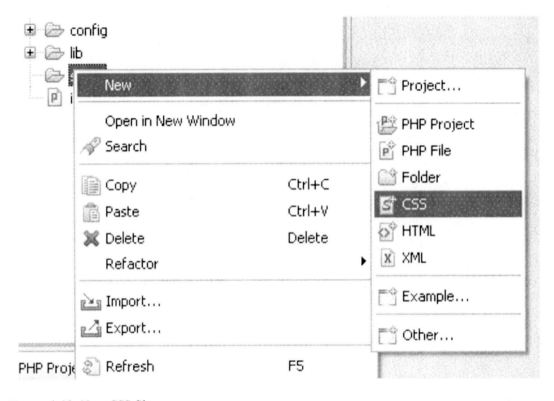

Figure 4-19. New CSS file

You don't have to make all the styles since Facebook takes care of many of these for you. However, for these purposes you'll develop your own. First, you need to provide some padding around your content, add a few Facebook-style boxes for your content, and add a wide left column and smaller right column for your containers.

You've already added some games into your database (some of my all-time favorites including Super Mario Brothers, Civilization II, The Legend of Zelda, and Half Life 2). Having placeholder data is really helpful in planning how the data will be viewed on the page, so the more data you have, the better.

You'll make your application better, but for the time being, your PHP calls to the database are in the index file. First for your box model, you wrap your content in a `<div>` tag, with an `id` of body. Next, for your canvas page, you want to have a wide left column (`left-wide`) and a small right column (`right-small`). Keeping with the general look and feel of the Facebook web site, you'll also have a few classes dedicated to displaying the header information in a consistent manner.

Using your PHP template, you produce the following for an initial view of your data:

```php
<?php
/**
 * File: index.php
 * Description: The index file of the application
 */

require_once('config/config.inc.php');

$conn = mysql_connect($database_server, $database_user, $database_password);
@mysql_select_db($database_name);

$review_sql = 'SELECT g.game_title, r.review_id, r.date_submitted,
    r.uid, review_counter.review_total
    FROM review r, game g,
        (
            SELECT count(*) AS review_total FROM review
        ) AS review_counter
    WHERE r.game_id = g.game_id
    ORDER BY date_submitted DESC
    LIMIT 5';

$recent_reviews = mysql_query($review_sql);
$review_count = mysql_fetch_row($recent_reviews);

$games_sql = 'SELECT * FROM game g ORDER BY added DESC LIMIT 5';
$recent_games = mysql_query($games_sql);

?>

<style>
<?php require_once('style/style.css'); ?>
</style>

<div id="body">
    <div id="left-wide">
        <div id="reviews">
            <!-- recent reviews -->
            <h2 class="header">Recent Reviews</h2>

            <div class="subheader clearfix">
                <div class="left">
                    <?php
                    echo('Displaying Latest 5 of ' . $review_count[4] );
```

```php
                echo(' Reviews');
            ?>
        </div>
        <div class="right">
            <a href="reviews.php">See all reviews</a>
        </div>

    </div>

    <div class="reviews box clearfix ">

        <?php
            while ($row = mysql_fetch_assoc($recent_reviews)) {
                echo('<div class="review clearfix">
                    <h3 class="review_title">
                        <a href="review.php?review_
                            id=' . $row['review_id']. '">'.
                                $row['game_title'] .
                        '</a>
                    </h3'
                );
                echo('<p class="more_info clearfix">Submitted ' .
                    $row['date_submitted'] . '</p></div>');
            }
        ?>
    </div>
</div>
</div>

<div id="right-small">
    <div class="box">
        <h2 class="header">recently added games</h2>
        <div class="subheader clearfix">
            <h3 style="float:right;">
                <a href="games.php">See all games</a>
            </h3>
        </div>
        <div class="clearfix">
            <?php
                while($row = mysql_fetch_assoc($recent_games)){
                    echo('<h3 class="game_info clearfix">
                        <a href="game.php?game_id=' . $row['game_id'] .'">'
                            . $row['game_title'] .
```

```
                                '</a></h3>');
                    }
            ?>
          </div>
        </div>
      </div>
</div>
```

You now have the initial design laid out, but you're also going to need some styles:

```css
#body {
    padding: 10px;
}

#left-wide{
    width: 406px;
    float: left;
}

#right-small {
    width: 210px;
    float: right;
}

.reviews{
    border-color:#EEEEEE;
    padding:7px 8px;
}

.review{
    border-color: #ccc;
    border-bottom:1px solid #CCCCCC;
    width: 100%;
}

.header {
    background: #D8DFEA none repeat scroll 0%;
    border-top: 1px solid #3B5998;
    margin: 0px;
    padding: 2px 8px;
}

.subheader {
    background: #eee none repeat scroll 0%;
```

```
        border-top: 1px solid #ccc;
        font-size: 12px;
        margin: 0px;
        padding: 2px 8px;
}

.subheader h3 {
        font-size: 11px;
        font-weight: normal;
}

.game_info {
        border-bottom:1px solid #ccc;
        float:left;
        padding:10px 10px 5px;
        width:170px;
}

.box {
        margin-bottom: 10px;
}

.more_info {
        float: left;
        padding-right: 10px;
        width: 340px;
}

.left{float:left}
.right{float:right}
```

If everything has gone correctly, you should now have something along the lines of Figure 4-20.

Recent Reviews		recently added games	
Displaying Latest 5 of 6 Reviews	See all reviews		See all games
Super Mario Brothers		Super Mario Brothers	
Submitted 2007-12-01 12:10:15		Civilization II	
The Legend of Zelda: A Link to the Past		The Legend of Zelda: Ocarina of Time	
Submitted 2007-12-01 12:10:15			
The Legend of Zeldo: Ocarina of Time		Super Mario 64	
Submitted 2007-12-01 12:10:15		Half-Life 2	
Super Mario 64			
Submitted 2007-12-01 12:10:15			

Figure 4-20. Initial Facebook view

Now that you have something up and running, you can deal with a few other initial details. For example, you need some type of method for users to actually add games and reviews to your application. For the purposes of this example, you'll write these as new pages that perform several different actions (list all the games/reviews, display individual games/reviews, and add a game/review).

Since there is a dependency on the existence of a game in the review table, let's start with the games page. You'll declare an action variable to control what is shown on the page, and then you'll use library functions to actually grab data for you. For the most part, I'm using the same conventions used by Facebook coders for consistency's sake.

Since you want to implement some code reuse, you'll first create a new file in the lib folder called dbmanager.php. You'll add useful functions to get data from your database here, along with some useful parameterization. The first thing you want to do is add some database configuration details to your config.inc.php file to store your database configuration details. At the end of the PHP file, add this section:

```
/*********************** Database Settings ***************************/
$database_server   = '<your_db_server>';
$database_user     = '<your_db_user>';
$database_password = '<your_db_password>';
$database_name     = '<your_db>';

$conn = mysql_connect($database_server, $database_user, $database_password);
@mysql_select_db($database_name);
```

This established a database connection that you can use to globally refer to other code segments in your application. Next you'll create a new PHP file as before in the `lib` folder named `dbmanager.php`. The first function you'll define is named query, which returns the results from your MySQL server for a given SQL command.

```
function query($sql){
    global $conn;
    return mysql_query($sql, $conn);
}
```

Now, you'll add the different queries you've already written. As with your main index page, you have a few queries that you can put into your dbmanager file so you can reuse these on different pages. These include the recent_reviews, review_count, game_count, and recent_games queries:

```
function get_recent_reviews($count){
    $query = query(sprintf('SELECT g.game_title, r.review_id, r.date_submitted,
                r.uid, review_counter.review_total
                FROM review r, game g,
                    (SELECT count(*) AS review_total FROM review)
                AS review_counter
                WHERE r.game_id = g.game_id
                AND 1
                ORDER BY date_submitted DESC
                LIMIT %d', $count));

    return $query;
}

function get_review_count(){
    $query = query(sprintf('SELECT count(*) AS total_count FROM review'));

    if($row = mysql_fetch_assoc($query)){
    return $row['total_count'];
    }else {
    return 0;
    }
}

function get_game_count(){
    $query = query(sprintf('SELECT count(*) AS total_count FROM game'));

    if($row = mysql_fetch_assoc($query)){
```

```php
        return $row['total_count'];
    } else {
        return 0;
    }
}

function get_recent_games($count){
    $query = query(sprintf('SELECT *
                FROM game
                ORDER BY added DESC
                LIMIT %d', $count));
    return $query;
}
```

You'll notice in this code that you parameterize the input through the sprintf function, just to keep those hackers a little more honest. Each of these will return a mysql_result object. You use these as you would any other mysql_result object with normal loop constructs. Let's update the code on your main index page to use these new functions. Just use the require_once construct to include the dbmanager.php file. Now, return to the index.php file where you have defined the call to the MySQL file, and replace the contents of the file with calls to these functions:

```php
<?php
/**
 * File: index.php
 * Description: The index file of the application
 */

require_once('config/config.inc.php');
require_once('lib/dbmanager.php');

$recent_reviews = get_recent_reviews(5);
$review_count = get_review_count();

$recent_games = get_recent_games(5);
$game_count = get_game_count();

?>
```

Since you used the same variable names, the rest of the code on the page doesn't change, and you have cleaner code.

Now let's create a couple of functions to retrieve game information. You want to be able to deal with all games and a single game, so you'll create two more functions in the dbmanager.php file to deal with each of these cases. The get_all_games function will take no parameters, and the get_game function will require a game_id parameter.

```php
function get_all_games(){
    $query = query(sprintf('SELECT * FROM game ORDER BY added DESC'));

    return $query;
}

function get_game($game_id){
    $query = query(sprintf('SELECT * FROM game WHERE game_id = %d', $game_id));

    return $query;
}
```

Now that you can actually get some data from your database, let's make some displays in the games.php file. You create this file with the same procedure as before. The code will be a bit more complicated, so let's deal with displaying all_games first. In your games.php file, let's declare a variable $action that will tell the script what to do and then add skeleton if/else if statements.

```php
<?php
/**
 * File: games.php
 * Description: Page for handling games
 */
require_once('config/config.inc.php');
require_once('lib/dbmanager.php');

if(isset $_REQUEST('action'){
    $action = $_REQUEST('action');
} else {
    $action = 'showall';
}
?>

<style>
<?php require_once('style/style.css'); ?>
</style>

<div id="body">

<?php
```

Graham

```
if($action == 'display'){
    // show all games in the collection

} else if($action == 'add'){
    // form to add new game

} else {
    // show all games in the collection

}
?>
</div>
```

For your default action (that displays all the games), you'll simply call the get_all_games function from your dbmanager.php include file and do some formatting. Insert the following code in the else block of the if($action == 'showall') statement:

```
} else {
    $all_games = get_all_games();

    print('<div id="games">');

    while ($row = mysql_fetch_array($all_games)){
        $game_rating = get_game_rating($row['game_id']);

        $title = $row['game_title'];
        $game_id = $row['game_id'];
        $publisher = $row['publisher'];
        $year = $row['release_year'];
        $rating = $row['esrb_rating'];
        $added = date('d M, Y', strtotime($row['added']));

        echo <<<EOT
<div class="game">
    <div class="game_about">
        <p class="game_header">
            <a href="games.php?game_id=$game_id&action=display">
                $title
            </a>
            by $publisher ($year)
        </p>
        <p><strong>ESRB Rating:</strong> $rating</p>
```

```
        <p><strong>Added:</strong> $added</p>
        <p><a href="games.php?action=display&game_id=$game_id">see reviews</a></p>
    </div>
    <div class="bumper" />
</div>
EOT;
    }

        print('</div>');
}
```

You'll notice here I'm using heredoc notation to save some typing. You could have also used print or echo, but I find that heredoc is far easier to read, especially when writing a block of output. You'll also notice that I added a few new classes to the style sheet.

```
#games {
    padding: 10px;
}

.game {

}

.bumper {
    background:#D8DFEA none repeat scroll 0%;
    border:medium none;
    color:#D8DFEA;
    height:1px;
    margin-bottom: 21px;
    overflow:hidden;
    clear: both;
}

.game_header {
    font-size: 13px;
}

.game_header a{
    font-weight: bold;
}
```

Now, if you navigate to the games web page, you'll see something along the lines of Figure 4-21.

Super Mario Brothers by Nintendo (1995)

ESRB Rating: E

Added: 10 Dec, 2007

see reviews

Resident Evil 4 by Capcom (2005)

ESRB Rating: M

Added: 10 Dec, 2007

see reviews

Final Fantasy III by Square (1994)

ESRB Rating: E 10+

Added: 10 Dec, 2007

see reviews

The Legend of Zelda: A Link to the Past by Nintendo (1992)

ESRB Rating: E

Added: 10 Dec, 2007

see reviews

Figure 4-21. Listing of games

Adding an average rating and the number of reviews for each game is also very easy. Just write a new function in dbmanager.php to grab the information from the database for each of the elements:

```
function get_game_rating($game_id){
    $query = query(sprintf('SELECT avg(rating) AS game_rating
                    FROM review WHERE game_id = %d', $game_id));

    if($row = mysql_fetch_assoc($query)){
        return round($row['game_rating']);
    } else {
        return 0;
    }
}

function get_game_review_count($game_id){
    $query = query(sprintf('SELECT count(*) AS review_count
                        FROM review WHERE game_id = %d', $game_id));

    if($row = mysql_fetch_assoc($query)){
        return $row['review_count'];
    } else {
        return 0;
    }
}
```

Your display should now incorporate this new data, but wouldn't it be nice if you could incorporate those little rating stars instead of having a number? The get_game_rating function returns a rounded average, so you just need to get some stars. I made my own stars, but if you don't know how to do this, there are plenty of tutorials online (just Google *star rating tutorial*). The basic idea here is that a rating can be from 0 (not rated) to 5 (the highest rating). You make a file for each of these, and you basically just use the <img> FBML tag. Remember, the <img> tag in Facebook requires an absolute reference; no relative URLs are allowed. In other words, you must put the entire path to your image, as in http://www.foobar.com/facebook/images/1.png.

External Web Services

Another nice feature you might want to include is pictures of the covers for the different games you're reviewing. Fortunately, you don't have to store these images yourself; you can use Amazon's Amazon Web Service (AWS) to pull the appropriate images into your application. To use this great service, you'll need an AWS access key from Amazon. If you don't already have one, you can sign up at http://aws.amazon.com/. I'll cover joining the associate program in the next chapter, but for the time being, you just need an AWS access key.

Since you'll probably want to use this on many pages, make a global variable for the key in the config.inc.php file:

```
/********************* Amazon Settings **************************/
$amazon_key = '<your_amazon_aws_key>';
```

Now you'll create a new file named amazon.php in your lib folder to handle your calls to Amazon's web service. This is a very basic class object that will work through Amazon's REST protocol to query specific XML responses.

```php
<?php
class AmazonClient {
    public $amazon_key;          // AWS key
    public $amazon_associate;    // associate id, if you have one

    public function __construct($amazon_key, $amazon_associate=''){
        $this->amazon_key = $amazon_key;
        $this->amazon_associate = $amazon_associate;
    }

    /**
     * Simple REST client for Amazon AWS
     * @param $params Query parameters to pass to AWS
     * @return SimpleXML object of the REST response
     */
    function amazon_search($params){
        $url = $this->build_query($params);

        $response = file_get_contents($url);

        $xmlObject = simplexml_load_string($response);

        return $xmlObject;
    }

    /**
     * Function to build query string for AWS
     * @param $params search parameters to pass to AWS
     * @return AWS REST query URL string
     */
```

```php
function build_query($params){
    $constants = array('Service' => 'AWSECommerceService',
                       'SubscriptionId' => $this->amazon_key,
                       'AssociateTag' => $this->amazon_id,
                       'SearchIndex' => 'VideoGames');

    $query_string = '';

    // add params to search string
    foreach($constants as $key => $value){
        $query_string .= "$key=" . urlencode($value) . "&";
    }

    // add searchparams to search string
    foreach($params as $key => $value){
        $query_string .= "$key=" . urlencode($value) . "&";
    }

    return = 'http://ecs.amazonaws.com/onca/xml?' . $query_string;
}

/**
 * Return an array of the images (small, medium,
 *     and large) for a given ASIN
 * @param $asin The ASIN number to search
 */
function get_game_image($asin){
    $params = array( 'Keywords' => $asin,
                     'Operation' => "ItemSearch",
                     'ResponseGroup' => 'Images' );

    $xml = $this->amazon_search($params);

    $results = array();

    foreach($xml->Items->Item as $item){

        $results['small_url'] = $item->SmallImage->URL;
        $results['small_height'] = $item->SmallImage->Height;
        $results['small_width'] = $item->SmallImage->Width;

        $results['medium_url'] = $item->MediumImage->URL;
        $results['medium_height'] = $item->MediumImage->Height;
```

```
                $results['medium_width'] = $item->MediumImage->Width;

                $results['large_url'] = $item->LargeImage->URL;
                $results['large_height'] = $item->LargeImage->Height;
                $results['large_width'] = $item->LargeImage->Width;
        }

        return $results;
    }

}
?>
```

Tip ➡ Not sure what's needed in your AWS call? There's a great online resource at `http://www.awszone.com` that lists all the fields you can search for a given search type. If you run into problems, just fill out the form and see what needs to be in your URL when searching the AWS servers.

Now, all you need to do is include the class, instantiate the object, and call the get_game_image method. But wait…that method requires a field called ASIN that you haven't added to your database. Let's commit this new tuple to the game table and work on fixing what you have so far.

First you'll add the field to the database using the Database Development tool. If you open the SQL file you created earlier (or a new one) and set your connection information, you may notice that your database isn't selected. To see your database, you have to connect to the database system. You can do this by switching to the Database Development view, right-clicking your database instance, and selecting Connect (see Figure 4-22).

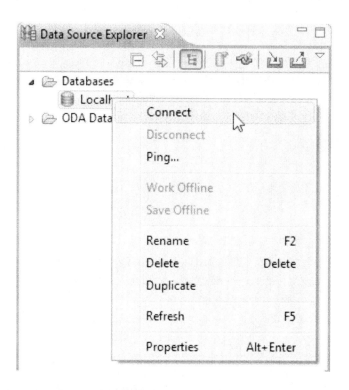

Figure 4-22. Reconnecting to your database back end

Once you have an SQL file open, modify the table definition with this:

```
ALTER TABLE game ADD COLUMN asin VARCHAR(30) NOT NULL AFTER release_year;
```

This adds the new ASIN tuple into to the database, but you still need to get the ASINs (where they exist) for the rest of the games. For convenience, I looked these up already, and you can just update the game table with the following. We'll deal with looking up ASINs when new games are added.

```
UPDATE game SET asin = 'B0001ZZNNI' WHERE game_id = 1;
UPDATE game SET asin = 'B000B69E9G' WHERE game_id = 2;
UPDATE game SET asin = 'B000GABOTU' WHERE game_id = 3;
UPDATE game SET asin = 'B000B69E9G' WHERE game_id = 4;
UPDATE game SET asin = 'B00002STXN' WHERE game_id = 5;
UPDATE game SET asin = 'B00002SVFV' WHERE game_id = 6;
UPDATE game SET asin = 'B000ID1AKI' WHERE game_id = 7;
UPDATE game SET asin = 'B00000DMB3' WHERE game_id = 8;
UPDATE game SET asin = 'B000FPM8OG' WHERE game_id = 9;
UPDATE game SET asin = 'B000W1XGW6' WHERE game_id = 10;
```

```
UPDATE game SET asin = 'BOOOFRUONU' WHERE game_id = 11;
```

I like how Amazon displays its images, so let's put the small image from AWS on the games page. Now, include the new Amazon page, and call the code:

```
$require_once('lib/amazon.php');
$amazon = new AmazonClient($amazon_key);
$images = $amazon->get_game_image($row['asin']);

// make sure a structure was returned
if(sizeof($images) > 0){
    $image = $images['small_url'];
    $img = '<img src="' . $image . '" />';
} else {
    $img = 'No Image Available';
}
```

Now you just need to edit the heredoc string to include a new <div> for the image in the games.php file:

```
<div class="game_image">
    $img
</div>
```

Lastly, add a bit of CSS to define the game_image style and then update the game_about style to clear the image style:

```
.game_image {
    float: left;
}

.game_about {
    margin-left: 60px;
}
```

Let's take a look at your work now. If everything has gone to plan, you should now have something that looks like Figure 4-23.

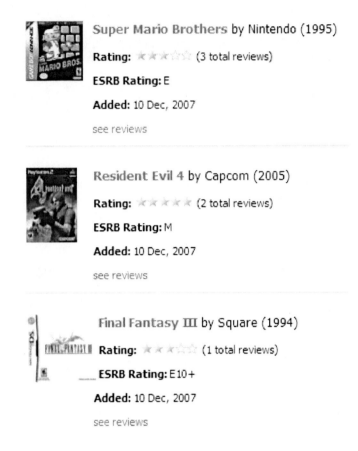

Figure 4-23. Games view with images

Game Review

You're quickly getting a useful application together. Now you'll build the individual game review page. You need to write a new query to get all the reviews with a specified game_id. In the dbmanager.php file, add the following function:

```
function get_game_reviews($game_id){
    $query = query(sprintf('SELECT * FROM review r WHERE game_id = %d
                 ORDER BY date_submitted DESC', $game_id));

    return $query;
}
```

This function simply gets all the information from the review table for the game_id. Since you have constructed the URL for the action already, you can grab the actual game information as you did in the previous loop structure by including the following code in the games.php file:

```php
if(! isset($_REQUEST['game_id'])){
    $_REQUEST['game_id'] = 1;
}

$game_id = $_REQUEST['game_id'];
$game = get_game($game_id);

$game_rating = get_game_rating($game_id);
$game_reviews = get_game_reviews($game_id);

$title = $game['game_title'];
$game_id = $game['game_id'];
$publisher = $game['publisher'];
$year = $game['release_year'];
$rating = $game['esrb_rating'];
$added = date('d M, Y', strtotime($game['added']));

$game_rating = get_game_rating($game_id);
$review_count = get_game_review_count($game_id);

$amazon = new AmazonClient($amazon_key);
$images = $amazon->get_game_image($game['asin']);

if(sizeof($images) > 0){
    $image = $images['medium_url'];
    $img = '<img src=' . $image. " />";
} else {
    $img = 'No Image Available';
}

echo <<<EOT
<div class="game">
    <div class="game_image">
        $img
    </div>
    <div class="game_about_medium">
        <p class="game_header">
            <a href="games.php?game_id=$game_id&action=display">
```

```
            $title
        </a>
        by $publisher ($year)
    </p>
    <p>
        <strong>Rating:</strong>
        <img src="<your_path_to_images>/$game_rating.png"
            alt="$game_rating" title="Average rating of $game_rating" />
                ($review_count total reviews)
    </p>
    <p><strong>ESRB Rating:</strong> $rating</p>
    <p><strong>Added:</strong> $added</p>
    </div>
    <div class="bumper" />
</div>
EOT;
```

This gives you the primary game description (along with a new offset style class that sets the left margin of the information to 160 pixels since we're using the medium-sized image), so let's take it a step further and add the review information. You'll style the reviews basically like a wall, with newer posts at the top:

```
print('<div id="reviews">');

while($row = mysql_fetch_assoc($game_reviews)){
    $uid = $row['uid'];
    $rating = $row['rating'];
    $review = nl2br($row['review']);
    $submitted = strtotime($row['date_submitted']);

    $time = date('h:ia', $submitted);
    $date = date('d M, Y', $submitted);
    $stars = '<your_callback_url>/images/' . $rating . '.png';

    echo <<< EOT
<div class="review">
    <div class="userimage">
        <fb:profile-pic uid="$uid" linked="true" size="q" />
    </div>

    <div class="review_box">
        <div class="review_header">
            <fb:name uid="$uid" capitalize="true" linked="true" /> reviewed
```

```
                <strong>$title</strong> <br/>
                    at $time on $date
        </div>
        <div class="review_text">
            <p>$review</p>
            <p><img src="$stars" /></p>
        </div>
    </div>
</div>
EOT;
```

For the reviews, this code used the `<fb:name>` and `<fb:profile-pic>` to pull in user data (including links to the user profiles). You could have made a more sophisticated FQL query to find the user's information (name and picture), but using the tags is far more efficient, especially since these tags were designed specifically to do what you're doing here.

Add Game

The last thing you need to do for this page is allow people to add new games to your application, so here you'll start coding the "add" section. For this action, you'll use MockAjax to add information to the form. You could also use the `<fb:editor>` tag (or just a plain old HTML form), but the MockAjax facilities for adding a modal dialog box are nice to work with.

You'll be nesting your form within the `<fb:dialog>` tag. The nice part about this is that you can put this anywhere on your page, and it will be hidden until someone clicks an action item (for example, a hyperlink) that has a `clicktoshowdialog` attribute. You'll then use the power of FBJS to insert the information into the database and refresh the game page.

To start, you'll add a couple of links inside the body `<div>`. The first one just returns you to the default view, and the other sets up the call to the dialog box. In the body `<div>`, add the following lines:

```
<a href="games.php">all games</a>
<a href="#" clicktoshowdialog="add_game">add game</a>
```

Now you'll add the actual dialog box that get called when the user clicks the Add Game link:

```
<fb:dialog id="add_game" cancel_button="1">
    <fb:dialog-content>
        <form id="add_game_form" method="post" action="add_game.php">
            <table>
```

```
            <tr>
                <td>Game Title:</td>
                <td><input type="text" name="game_title" /></td>
            </tr>
            <tr>
                <td>Publisher:</td>
                <td><input type="text" name="publisher" /></td>
            </tr>
            <tr>
                <td>Year Released:</td>
                <td><input type="text" name="release_year" /></td>
            </tr>
            <tr>
                <td>Rating:</td>
                <td>
                    <select name="esrb_rating">
                        <option value="EC">EC</option>
                        <option value="E" selected>E</option>
                        <option value="E10+">E10+</option>
                        <option value="T">T</option>
                        <option value="M">M</option>
                        <option value="AO">AO</option>
                    </select>
                </td>
            </tr>
        </table>
    </form>
</fb:dialog-content>

    <fb:dialog-button type="submit" value="Add Game" form_id="add_game_form" />

</fb:dialog>
```

Because you're using the `<fb:dialog>` tag, the form will be shown only when the user clicks the Add Game hyperlink. You pass the entire form a new page (add_game.php) that contains the logic to add games to the application by referencing the form_id in the `<fb:dialog>` tag. The code in add_game.php will handle looking up the ASIN of the game from Amazon, inserting the data, and redirecting the user to the games.php page with a status message.

You'll need to add a couple of functions in the dbmanager.php and AmazonRestClient code. In the AmazonRestClient, you need a function that will look up an ASIN for a given title. In the dbmanager.php code, you have a couple of functions, one to tell you whether a given title has already been inserted in the database and one to insert data into the database.

Graham

To write the ASIN lookup, you need to retrieve information for a title lookup. This will be a fairly basic lookup where you assume that the first result passed back from Amazon is the correct title the person was inserting. In a more sophisticated application, you want to present the results to the user to let them choose which title they actually wanted.

```php
function asin_lookup($title){
    $params = array('Title' => $title, 'Operation' => 'ItemSearch',
                    'ResponseGroup' => 'ItemAttributes');

    $xml = $this->amazon_search($params);

    $xml_result = $xml->Items->Item;

    return $xml_result->ASIN;
}
```

Now all that is left is a little checking in the add_game.php page to make sure everything went OK. First, you want to make sure that the game title doesn't exist in the database, and then you look up the ASIN and insert the new game record into the database:

```php
if(isset($_REQUEST['game_title'])){
    $game_title = $_REQUEST['game_title'];

    $type = "error";

    if(game_exists($game_title)){
        // check to see if the title exists
        $message = "Sorry, looks like " . $game_title .
            " is already in our database";
    } else {
        // check in Amazon
        $amazon = new AmazonClient($amazon_key);

        $asin = $amazon->asin_lookup($game_title);

        if(strlen($asin) > 0){
            // double-check this in the database

            if(game_exists_asin($asin)){
                $message = "Sorry, looks like " . $game_title;
                $message += " is already in our database";
            } else {
                add_game($_REQUEST['game_title'], $_REQUEST['publisher'],
```

```
                  $_REQUEST['release_year'], $_REQUEST['esrb_rating'],
                  $asin);
          $message = $_REQUEST['game_title'] . " was successfully added";
          $message +=  " to the database.  Please be sure to write a
review!";
          $type = "success";
      }
  } else {
      $message = "Sorry, couldn't find " . $_REQUEST['game_title'];
      $message += " at Amazon.";
  }
}

echo('<fb:redirect url="games.php?message=' . urlencode($message)
    . '&type=' . $type . '" />');

}
```

This code will return a status message in the games.php page that lets the user know whether a game was added, as well as other information. If a new game was successfully added, that fact is sent to the user's profile, and the user is then redirected to the games.php page. The last thing you want to do at the top of the games.php page is display the message from the add_game.php code.

Just under the navigation in games.php, add this code to display the messages:

```
<?php
    if(isset($_GET['message'])){
        if($_GET['type'] == "success"){
            echo('<fb:success message="' . $_GET['message'] . '"/>');
        } else {
            echo('<fb:error message="' . $_GET['message'] . '"/>');
        }
    }
?>
```

This is just a nice way to give the user a little feedback on successful/unsuccessful actions.

You've done the heavy-lifting for your application; now the reviews are a piece of cake. I won't go into great detail for this since I've covered most of the techniques before. Instead of filling these pages with code, I'm certain you can write the rest of the code for this application.

Graham

Publishing Feeds

Now that you have a functioning application, one further improvement is to publish the actions to the user's profile. There are really two way you can do this. The first is to publish to the individual's feed, and the other is to publish to the user's friends' feeds. The fun part is to use `feed.publishTemplatizedAction` to publish a templatized action to the user's feed.

For any action you want to immortalize in your user's feed, simply call the `feed_publishTemplatizedAction` function from the `FacebookRestClient` object:

```
$title_template = '{actor} added {game} to MyTestApp';

$title_data = '{"game":"' . $game_title .'"}';

$facebook->api_client->feed_publishTemplatizedAction($title_template,
    $title_data, '', '', '');
```

I especially like to publish feeds this way because the feed preview from the Facebook tools (`http://developers.facebook.com/tools.php?feed`) gives you a lot of help in testing how the feed will look. The big thing to remember is that you need to have {actor} somewhere in the `$title_template` variable so Facebook knows where to place the proper username in the text. This tag did go through a recent change, so make sure you take a look at the most recent wiki documents for the latest on this tag.

Testing

You'll need to create a new account (not your real account) on Facebook and then register that account as a test user at `http://www.facebook.com/developers/become_test_account.php`. You'll need an e-mail address for this account to work, so you can create one at Google, Yahoo, or MSN, or you can create e-mail aliases with a service such as MailExpire (`http://www.mailexpire.com/`). You should remember that test users aren't "real" Facebook users, so they won't see the "real" people on the network. Also, you can't set a test account to be the application owner.

You most likely need only one of these accounts to test your application (or ask a good friend). However, this doesn't actually provide you with any real human input. If you want to get some "real" people to give you some feedback, there's a channel in the forums to do this (`http://forum.developers.facebook.com/viewforum.php?id=16`). Remember, these folks are volunteering their time to give you feedback. If their feedback isn't what you're expecting, remember to stay positive because we've all seen forums degrade quickly into name calling.

Graham

Debugging

So, what if you run into a problem and something just isn't displaying properly in your application? There are a bunch of tools that can help. Chief among these are the error messages that you get on your page. In case you've forgotten a = or ; in your code, you can at least see the line that you need to check. Another handy tool is the Firebug extension for Firefox (`http://www.getfirebug.com/`), especially if you're working with FBJS and MockAjax. The JavaScript console can give you important details on what's going on, plus it's great for dissecting code and CSS. If you don't already have it, I highly recommend downloading this extension ASAP!

Facebook also has tools to help you isolate your code and test it. The Tools page on the Facebook Developers web site (`http://developer.facebook.com/tools.php`) has several tools that are useful in figuring out (and testing) how code will look/function in the wild.

If you still are running into problems, you can turn to the Facebook forums (`http://forum.developers.facebook.com/`). You can search for your particular problem or start a new thread. There are also IRC channels for chatting with other Facebook developers (such as `#Facebook` on freenode). More often than not, someone hanging out in one of these areas can at least point you in the correct direction. Remember, be clear and concise when you're describing your problem; subjects like "My app is broken" probably won't get much helpful feedback.

Scaling

So, what happens when you write an application that has 500,000 installations and huge bandwidth constraints? I hope you've placed some ads somewhere that will offset your server costs, or you may get kicked off your server host. Watch your apps, and if you need to get more bandwidth, see whether your provider has larger plans.

Not that this is necessarily an endorsement, but Joyent recently announced a deal to provide its Accelerator service free for one year to Facebook developers (`http://www.joyent.com/developers/facebook`). Its basic service offers at least one processor and 512 megabytes of RAM with 10GB of storage with no bandwidth restrictions. There is a waiting list now, but it is an option to get you off the ground. If you outgrow these parameters, there are also plans starting at $45/month. Again, I can't stress this enough: if your application doesn't have the capacity to grow with your users, people will start removing your application, and no one wants that to happen!

Launching Your Application

Although launching a Facebook application is relatively easy (you just allow people to add the application and submit it to Facebook to be listed), there are several last considerations before releasing your code into the wild.

Creating the About Page

The About page is where your users first learn about your application. A concise explanation of your application and what it does is important, but you also need to catch your potential user's attention. For instance, there are a set of popular Facebook applications that extend the default functionality of Facebook. These have names like SuperPoke, Super Wall, and Top Friends. Give your application name some thought. Be clever, but not too clever as to obfuscate the true nature of your application.

Your About page also has several sections that you need to visit (or subscribe to). The forums are a great place for people to ask you about what's going on, how to improve the application, and what to do when things aren't clearly planned out in a logical fashion. These are a great way for you to communicate with your users, but remember, Facebook users can, at times, be fickle, so they will most likely just uninstall your application if they don't find it useful.

Creating a Logo

Designing a logo can be a bear for programmers (just like programming can be a chore for designers). At the least, you should be able to implement a Web 2.0 badge (there are a lot of online versions of these generators). If your icon version doesn't look right, there are several open source icon libraries. Tango's Icon Library (`http://tango.freedesktop.org/Tango_Icon_Library`) and FamFamFam's Silk Icons (`http://www.famfamfam.com/lab/icons/silk/`) are two popular sets that you can use in your application.

If you're a designer, the sky is the limit. Just make sure you have images for all the different sizes that can go into different areas of the web site (from 16 X 16 on up). There aren't really any guidelines, but be aware that any image published through the Facebook platform gets cached on Facebook's server. If you update your image and it doesn't immediately take (and you're impatient like I am), call the `facebook.fbml.refreshImgSrc` API method (for example, `$facebook->api_client->fbml_refreshImgSrc($image_url)` function).

Graham

Submitting for Approval

Once you're finished with your application, it's time to submit it to the Facebook approvers. Log on to the Developer application (`http://www.facebook.com/developers/apps.php`), and edit your settings so that everyone can add your application. Then simply click the Submit Application button.

It generally takes a few days for the people who approve applications to respond. They're looking at the application to make sure it's appropriate for their terms of service (in case you forgot to read them, here's the link `http://www.facebook.com/developers/tos.php`). After it's been approved, people will be able to find your application on the main application page (`http://www.facebook.com/apps/`).

Publicizing Your Application

Facebook is a viral community. The first step in getting folks to use your application is to get your friends to start using your application. Then, you need to get your friends to tell their friends about the application. However, you can also get others by purchasing Social Ads from Facebook (`http://www.facebook.com/business/?socialads`).

Advanced Techniques

When you start developing applications, you'll notice that there are a lot of things that you do repeatedly. For instance, for every application you create, you'll be coding the inserting, deleting, update, and reading of the data in your tables. After a while, this can become annoying. This is where the various frameworks come into play. CakePHP and symfony are two popular PHP web application frameworks that can easily be integrated into your Facebook application. These frameworks remove a layer of monotony from developing, allowing you to focus your efforts on developing "real" code, rather than repetitive SQL statements, confusing conditional statements in your pages, and implementing MVC patterns to "simplify" your code. If you haven't taken some time to sit down with either of these, it is well worth it because they will save you time in future development.

Another element to explore is migrating your data to Facebook's Data Store API. By using Facebook to store your data (and back it up), you have access to Facebook's scalable data storage servers. You may also want to look at Amazon's SimpleDB, but you should probably start with Facebook unless you have objections to Facebook "owning" the data for your application.

Graham

Summary

We covered a lot of ground in this chapter. You created an application all the way from start to finish using Eclipse, MySQL, PHP, and the Facebook platform. I discussed some of the issues you can run into when developing an application and how to deal with code that's not behaving as expected. Although I didn't walk you completely through the code to post reviews, you should know enough to complete this on your own very quickly (or build upon it for your own application).

In the next, final chapter, I'll go over some ways to track how many people are using your application and how you can turn this into a little extra revenue.

CHAPTER 5

Going Further with Your Application

In previous chapters, I covered the meat and potatoes of creating Facebook applications. In this chapter, I'll shift the focus a bit to the salt and pepper by covering the resources that you can use to analyze your application statistics, where to go if you get stuck, and, perhaps most important, how to generate a revenue stream from your application! Although some applications have sold for quite a bit of money and some generate a good revenue stream from advertisements, it's important to remember that most likely you're not going to make a $1,000,000 with your Facebook application, because many mitigating circumstances contribute to the success of turning an application into a blockbuster. However, with some planning and some good choices, you should be able to at least offset the costs of your server hosting.

Application Statistics

Facebook provides a basic statistics feature in the Facebook Developer application to help you get an idea of what's going on with your application. These statistics include usage statistics, HTTP status requests, and recent HTTP requests. Within the usage statistics, you are provided with a helpful User Engagement statistic that tells you how many people used your application in the past 24 hours. Although the total number of users of an application may be quite high, this engagement number is important because it helps you figure out how many people are actually "using" your application. If this number isn't very high, chances that the application will be able to sustain itself are reasonably low.

What if you need or want more sophisticated statistics? This is where the `<fb:google-analytics>` tag comes in handy. You will need to create an account on Google Analytics to use this tag, but it's quite simple to use, and it provides exceptionally detailed statistics about your application (and for that matter, any web site you might build).

If you don't already have a Google Analytics account, navigate to `http://www.google.com/analytics/`. You need a Google account to use Google Analytics, so if you don't already have one, you can sign up by clicking the Sign Up Now link in the middle of the page, as shown in Figure 5-1.

The New Google Analytics
Google Analytics has been re-designed to help you learn even more about where your visitors come from and how they interact with your site.

Discover. Share. Act.
The new Google Analytics makes it easy to improve your results online. Write better ads, strengthen your marketing initiatives, and create higher-converting websites. Google Analytics is free to all advertisers, publishers, and site owners.

Sign Up Now

Figure 5-1. Google Analytics sign-up link

Once you have an account set up, the next step is to add a web site profile. Simply click the Add Website Profile link after logging in to start the process. Then fill out the form for a new domain using your server URL (not your http://apps.facebook.com/<your_app_name> URL), as shown in Figure 5-2, and click Continue.

Choose Website Profile Type

Please decide if you would like to create an additional profile for an existing domain, or create a profile to track a new domain.

◉ Add a Profile for a **new** domain   OR   ○ Add a Profile for an **existing** domain

Add a Profile for a new domain

Please provide the URL of the site you would like to track.

http:// [▼] www.mywebsite.com/facebook

Examples: www.mywebsite.com
Note: You can add more profiles after you add this profile

Time zone country or territory: United States   [▼]
Time zone: (GMT-05:00) Eastern Time   [▼]

[Cancel] [**Continue**]

Figure 5-2. Google Analytics site registration

Graham

After you've registered your site, you're presented with a small snippet of JavaScript to add to your page. But wait, you can't use this because it's not FBJS! So, just get the account number (defined by the _uacct variable) to use the <fb:google-analytics> tag, and let Facebook write this in for you (see Figure 5-3).

```
<script src="http://www.google-analytics.com/urchin.js" type="text/javascript">
</script>
<script type="text/javascript">
_uacct = "UA-68867-7";
urchinTracker();
</script>
```

Figure 5-3. Google-provided source code including Google Analytics account number

Now, in your application, you merely add the following to produce the required JavaScript in your application:

```
<fb:google-analytics uacct="<your_UA_account_number>" />
```

When used in your application, Facebook will add the correct JavaScript to the resultant HTML stream. You may even want to define this in a global include (just in case you write a new page and forget to add the code to track its usage).

You also have access to the Google Analytics tracker in FBJS with the Facebook.urchinTracker object in case you need it. Most of the time it will be a lot easier to use the <fb:google-analytics> tag than to implement your own methods through FBJS; however, should you need more granular control over what gets sent to the Google servers for your application, the functionality does exist.

Once you've added the tag to your application, it typically takes about 24 hours for an update to occur and for you to see any statistics. Google Analytics will provide you with a really great statistics set including a site overlay (you want to make sure your features/ads are properly placed), geotargeting (to see where your users are from), Google AdWords integration, and just about any other type of useful statistic that you could possibly want about the people using your application.

Monetizing

Facebook has worked into its service agreements to allow application developers to monetize their applications. When you start looking at the different options available to you, you may find rather quickly that your head starts spinning from the sheer volume of advertising alternatives. The following is a brief treatment of some of the more popular ways developers have helped defray their costs.

AdSense

Since you've set up a Google Analytics account, it's not that much more effort to enable Google AdSense. You first go to the AdSense web site at http://adsense.google.com. You'll notice that if you're signed in to other Google services (Gmail, iGoogle, Analytics, and so on), you'll still need to create a separate AdSense account. Simply click the large Sign Up Now button (if you don't already have an account). Don't worry, you are presented with the option to use your Google account information if you choose. After you've filled in the information needed in the application, it typically takes a day or two to be reviewed.

Once you've set up an AdSense account and filled out the appropriate tax forms, you need to decide what type of advertising you want to implement. Google provides ads for content, search, referrals, video, and mobile content. What your application is doing will drive your decision here. Since Facebook has implemented a really nice mobile version of its application, you can always use the mobile content in your application! Google also provides you with some options for your ads (text and images or text or images only), so once you've decided which one you want, choose a size and color palette that matches your overall application design.

Tip ➡ Blue Mix works well with the default Facebook color scheme.

You do need to make a small change to at least your main canvas page to get relevant ads from Google: you need to make it publicly available so it can be crawled by Google. Unfortunately, there's no <fb:adsense> tag (and there probably will never be one), so you have to hack your page a bit to make things work.

So, let's make your canvas page publicly visible. The big change from the code in the previous chapter is that you're no longer going to be using the require_login function in the Facebook object. You'll use the get_loggedin_user function instead:

```
// $user = $facebook->require_login();
$user = $facebook->get_loggedin_user();
```

Now, if you want to test whether a user is logged out, you can use this:

```
$is_logged_out = !$user;
```

Graham

You can use any of the canvas page tags on this page without any changes to your code, although you might need to refactor some of your existing code to see how it appears for non-logged-in users.

Now I'll discuss the iframe hack to use AdSense. You need to make a new page that contains the JavaScript that Google provides you when you generate the ads for your page on your web site, and then you need to call that page through the <fb:iframe> tag on your canvas page. So, let's say you've created a page on your site named ads.php and can get to the file at http://yoursite.com/ads.php. Now, simply insert the following where you want to place the ads:

```
<fb:iframe src="http://yoursite.com/ads.php" width="<google_ad_width>"
    height="<google_ad_height>" />
```

If you're having problems with relevant ads, you might also want to use Google hints. You'll need to edit the JavaScript code that AdSense provides you and define the google_hints variable with a comma-delimited list of keywords for your application. In other words, you'll want to hack your AdSense code to resemble something along the lines of this:

```
<script type="text/javascript"><!--
    google_ad_client = "pub-0000000000000000";
    google_hints = "keyword1, keyword2, keyword3,...";
    google_ad_slot = "0000000000";
    google_ad_width = 728;
    google_ad_height = 90;
//--></script>
<script type="text/javascript"
    src="http://pagead2.googlesyndication.com/pagead/show_ads.js">
</script>
```

The nice aspect of AdSense is that its ads are unobtrusive and can be placed nearly anywhere on a page. It also offers nice tools for tracking your earnings and growth over time. Although other sites might make you more money in the short run, AdSense has a proven ability to generate revenue, so you'll want to consider that when deciding what advertising folks to partner with.

Amazon

Amazon also has a great service to generate revenue streams in its Amazon Associates Web Service. You've already used part of Amazon's service to pull the images from Amazon, so in this instance you might be able to use this service to build specialized URLs to provide links to Amazon so users can purchase different games from the sample application (or anything else Amazon sells, for that matter).

Since you already have the ASIN stored in your database, you can easily generate a link to the store with your Associate's ID embedded in the link. The resulting anchor for the image brought in by the Amazon web service is as follows:

```
<a href="http://www.amazon.com/exec/obidos/ASIN/<asin>/<your_associate_id>">
    <img src="<path_to_image>"/>
</a>
```

This service won't work for every type of application. It works well for social review applications, but it might not work as well in other types. You may find that some of the widgets on the Affiliates web site (`https://affiliate-program.amazon.com/`) will work well for your application, and you'll notice that many of these widgets (under the Build Links/Widgets section) generate JavaScript. But again, the `<fb:iframe>` hack shown in the "AdSense" section is generally the recommended way to go.

Adonomics

Formally known as Appaholic, Adonomics provides "stock-market-style" analysis for your applications. This site provides a few different services. The first is a service to get people to install your application. There are multiple tiers of this that range from $5,000 to $480,000. If you're looking to build users for your application, this may very well be worth the cost. However, if you're thinking smaller, Adonomics also rents advertising space. This is great since Adonomics takes on finding the advertising clients for the different places in your application. To give some rough estimates, Adonomics claims an average of about $3.60 per user per year (about $0.30 per month per the number of active users for the previous month). Of course, your mileage may vary.

Others

You can use many of other services to generate revenue from your application. Although I can't get into all the various services in this book, here is a list of some others you might want to investigate:

- AdBrite (`http://www.adbrite.com`)

- Appsaholic (`http://apps.facebook.com/appsaholic/`)

- BannerConnect (`http://www.bannerconnect.net`)

- Chitika (http://chitika.com/facebookapi.php)

- Cubics (http://www.cubics.com)

- fbExchange (http://fbexchange.com)

- Neverblue (http://www.neverbluemedia.com)

- PeanutLabs (http://www.peanutlabs.com)

- Survey Savvy (http://www.surveysavvy.com)

- Zohark Ads (http://www.facebook.com/applications/Zohark_Ads/18584639088)

Developers have differing opinions about each of these companies, and being listing here isn't necessarily an endorsement (and if I've missed your company, I apologize). Rather, this is a list to help you get up to speed on the different companies that allow you to leverage their advertising in your application.

Advertising Tips

You may notice that there are some advertising strategies that work better on your site. If your users are all using Firefox with the Adblock add-on, most likely they won't see the advertising. Also, some agreements (such as the Google AdSense agreement) won't allow you to use multiple types of advertising. So, choose your advertising service carefully. Although it's a pain, it is important you read the terms of service carefully to fully understand what you're getting into. This can translate into some long and confusing reading, but having a good understanding of these terms will save you many headaches down the road.

Depending on your service agreement, you may or may not have much control on where your advertisements are placed. If you can, place your ads near rich media (that is, images) so that the user's eye is drawn to the resource. You will also want to integrate your advertising into the overall design; don't put in the ads as an afterthought! Here are some general rules (or perhaps, more accurately, observations) on what works:

- Ads at the top of the page do better than ads at the bottom.

- Ads near images and navigation do well since the user focuses on those areas.

- Ads that have long areas of text (that is, stories) do well placed at the bottom.

There are no hard-and-fast rules for integrating advertising into your web site. However, pay attention to what's going on through whatever tools your advertising supplier provides.

Graham

Selling Your Application

Another way to make some money from your application is to sell it. However, remember that the people you're selling it to are expecting to make more money off your application than they are paying you. You need to either build your application to maturity and show sustained growth or come up with some type of novel method that has a lot of promise. If you think you've built a killer application that has a lot more potential and, for whatever reason, want to sell your stake, here are a few places to start looking for a buyer:

- Altura (http://altura.com/)

- AppFactory (http://www.baypartners.com/appfactory/)

- EBay (http://www.ebay.com/)

Help, I'm Stuck! (and Other Resources)

So, you've gotten partway through your application, and there's this one little thing you just can't figure out how to implement. What do you do? Probably the single best resource for these types of problems is the Facebook Developers forum (or discussion board, depending on where you link from) at http://forum.developers.facebook.com/. If you're more comfortable on IRC, there's also a channel on freenode (#Facebook) where lots of folks hang out. This can (at times) be a faster way to get an answer to a specific question (though people may send you to the forums, so make sure you search them before you post a "n00b" question).

You may also want to check out the different Facebook developer groups (http://wiki.developers.facebook.com/index.php/Local_Developer_Group) or even ask questions at one of the Garage events (http://wiki.developers.facebook.com/index.php/Garage_Calendar).

Summary

Making a little bit of money on the side never hurt anyone, and in this chapter I briefly went over some avenues that are available to you as a Facebook developer to monetize your application. You saw how to easily integrate advertisements into your application with Google AdSense and how to use Amazon's affiliate program to help generate a revenue stream for your application.

Because Amazon and Google aren't the only players on the block, I also listed some other advertising agencies that many Facebook developers have used. It is important, however, to compare the different agreements to each other in order to find the right solution for your application. And, if you get to the point of wanting to sell your application, I listed a few avenues for you to pursue. Remember, the vast majority of applications don't create additional value to Facebook. If you want to sell your application, remember this altruism: Facebook isn't about content…it's about communication. Do something that Facebook lacks, or do it better than Facebook does it, and you'll be successful.

　　If you get stuck, remember that the forums and the wiki documentation are your friends. You can also drop me a line via Facebook (be sure to add me as a friend) with any comments. Good luck with your project!

Graham

Printed in the United States
115755LV00005B/36/P